Siberian Odyssey

SIBERIAN ODYSSEY

Richard Lysakowski, Ph.D.

VANTAGE PRESS
New York • Los Angeles

The source of the map on page 232 is unknown. The author has made a reasonable attempt to ascertain its origin. Anyone with information regarding this map, please contact the publisher.

FIRST EDITION

All rights reserved, including the right of reproduction in whole or in part in any form.

Copyright © 1990 by Richard Lysakowski, Ph.D.

Published by Vantage Press, Inc.
516 West 34th Street, New York, New York 10001

Manufactured in the United States of America
ISBN: 0-533-08386-9

Library of Congress Catalog Card No.: 89-90014

To Tadeusz
and thousands of others
who perished forever
and to those who survived
to give testimony
to the truth

Contents

Preface ix

1. Open the Door! 1
2. School Days 7
3. The Outbreak of War 23
4. Interrogations Begin 35
5. The Ultimate Test 52
6. Prison Life 63
7. The Long Journey 76
8. Camp Bureya 2—Can Anyone Survive? 94
9. False Freedom 117
10. Freedom at Last! 125
11. Shalom-Aleikom (Peace Be with You) 142
12. In the Polish Army 154
13. The Song of the Cornucopia 161
14. Return to the Land of the Living 166
15. Bronek's Story 169
16. May They Rest in Peace 184
17. Leaving the Land of Slavery—to Iran and Iraq 195
18. Great Britain—Service in the Allied Air Force 211
Epilogue 221

Appendix: Russia's Drive for Domination 225

Preface

My intention in writing this book was twofold. The first was a personal one, to fulfill a promise I made to a friend as he lay dying in my lap from hunger and exhaustion and to the many other fellow sufferers who perished in the Soviet slave labor camps. Relatively few eyewitness accounts have been published dealing with the Soviet political prisoners, even though there have been several "waves" in the deadly process of liquidation of opponents of the communist regime in Russia. This is for both the native Russian opponents of communism and the patriots from the many subjugated nations who could not give up their love for their faith or country. These people have not been acknowledged well at all. Searching through the library stacks I find that the ratio of books about the Nazi German extermination camps published after World War II to the works published about the Soviet "slow-death" camps in the vast subarctic regions was at least ten to one.

Nazi Germany was defeated at the end of World War II and was occupied largely by the Western Allies. Mass death camps at Dachau, Buchenwald, and Nordhausen and others were freed by the Western Allied troops. Thousands of documents were seized from the archives of prisons and execution camps. Also, many thousands of prisoners were saved whom the Germans had processed for gas chambers but had no time to execute. All those people had ghastly stories to tell, and thousands of documents were made available for the Nuremburg trials of Nazi war criminals. It was proven that upwards of 6 million innocent Jews and Slavs were ruthlessly killed by the Germans.

The USSR has large concentration camps from which not many have escaped to give testimony and information about the slave labor camps and prisons in this "inhuman land." The Russian communist regime has "liquidated" several times the number of people destroyed by the Nazis.

Soviet Russia was a partner of Nazi Germany in planning and starting World War II. The invasions of Poland, Lithuania, Latvia, Estonia, and several other countries in Central Europe were executed with close knowledge and cooperation of the two aggressors. When Nazi armies turned their guns against the Soviets in July of 1941, the Soviets had to look for help to the Western Allies, who were still fighting the Nazis on the western front. Thus at the end of WW II the Soviets found themselves on the victorious side and their own crimes and atrocities were not mentioned, so as not to spoil the "perfect" unity among the victors—or else because Stalin didn't want them mentioned. In fact, the Soviet generals sat as judges of their partners in crime at the Nuremberg trials in 1945. Representatives of Poland and other nations subjugated by the Red Army were not admitted to sit as judges.

In the Soviet prison system hardly any records were kept, and few were made public after WW II. The primary source of information concerning the political or "conscience" prisoners was what "leaked out" with those few people who survived. Even now, the unbelievably tight and total isolation of the whole punitive system in the USSR renders such leakages rare. Neither will the *glasnost* recently announced by Mr. Gorbachev allow the majority of that part of history to be "uncovered."

The second aim of my book is to present a historical background of Russian expansionism over a period of some four hundred years. The old tsarist imperialism reflected a simple but disguised urge to conquer other nations, best exemplified by the exploits and achievements of Tsar Peter I ("The Great"). There was no excuse given for that policy—just one man's crazy ambition to subjugate other people, of his own nation and other nations. Basically it wasn't much different from what Napoleon Bonaparte or Hitler wanted to do. If the invaded nation didn't like it, it was brutally suppressed and its citizens murdered anyway.

The current regime in Russia, with a sickle and hammer as its emblem, has for seventy years now preached the slogans about a one-class society of peasants and workers to its neighboring nations. These nations, however, have been steadily subjected to a policy of slow elimination, while the Moscow Politburo still insists that these are "People's Democracies."

This regime invaded, in partnership with the Nazi armies, its Polish neighbor and proclaimed all equally as "enemies of the people" Polish peasants, landowners and aristocracy, workers and merchants in the cities, clergy, lower level bureaucrats as well as the top government bureaucrats, schoolteachers and administrators, health and national safety service personnel, including the military, and even the poorest city dwellers. No social class was exempt. The Soviets equalized all social classes and treated them alike, both those who sympathized with communist philosophy in Poland and those who were against it. All members of the subjugated nation were not trusted, and many were arrested and imprisoned, even those who greeted the Red Army with flowers and helped them to calm the upset people after the treacherous invasion.

Such were the beginnings of the Polish People's Republic, which left an indelible imprint on my consciousness. No matter how far I am removed from those experiences, the evil injustices of the Soviet system keep on burning in my mind. This book is to keep people in the free world aware of what transpired in Soviet Russia in WW II and still persists today for unfortunates who dare to challenge their system.

Siberian Odyssey

1

Open the Door!

I awoke with a start. My heart pounded so violently I felt as though it would leap out of my chest. But I quickly realized that it was not just the beating of my heart that I heard. The hands on an old mechanical alarm clock standing on the corner shelf by the window indicated that it was 2:30 A.M. It was March 14, 1940. There was an insistent banging on the front door, repeated with brutal urgency, followed by the cry, "Open the door! This is the NKVD!"*

I saw my Aunt Frances, terrified beyond words, cautiously make her way through the short hallway from the kitchen to the front porch. Three soldiers banged on the door with heavy rifle butts as if they meant to break it down. When they heard the bolt slide, one soldier shoved the door open with his bayonet-tipped rifle barrel, almost knocking over my aunt. The three soldiers were suddenly in our kitchen, with rifles ready, and they herded the whole family into a corner. One of them, apparently the leader of the patrol, had typical Mongolian features—squinty

---

*Narodniy Komissariat Vnutriennyh Diel—The Ministry (Department) of Internal Affairs. In reality, it was a country-wide state secret police whose fine network of spies terrorized people throughout the USSR. It has existed in Russia ever since the reign of Tsar Peter the Great under various names: Opritchnina, Okhrana, Gendarmerie, Cheka, GPU, NKVD, MWD, and at present the KGB. All these names stood for approximately the same thing—the Department of Government Security.

eyes, wide flat cheeks, and a small nose. He spoke directly to me. "You Risha'rd?"

He spoke in Russian, but with a strange Asiatic accent, and I couldn't understand him because it didn't sound like my name and I was scared. Then he came closer, almost touching me, and again asked, "You Risha'rd?"

This time I couldn't say that I did not understand him. I answered in a weak, boyish voice, "Yes."

Then the patrol commander strongly motioned for me to go to the opposite wall. The rest of my family stood, frozen with fear. He ordered one of the soldiers to guard me, while the two others ransacked the house.

The search was very thorough. They started with the dining room, which was being used as a temporary sleeping room by my cousin Aleksandra, her husband Valdy, and their nine-month-old son. Moving very quickly, the two plunderers piled the contents of the portable wardrobe and all the drawers from every room in the middle of the floor. China, books, and kitchen utensils were also dumped onto the huge pile. Aleksandra barely managed to snatch up her infant son before the soldier turned to the crib and dumped its contents onto the pile.

During the search the soldier guarding us in the kitchen stood with the bayonet pointed directly at me. He was ready to shoot or stab me if I made any sudden move. I knew he meant business by the vicious look in his eyes. His menacing, arrogant pose indicated that he saw something in me that he didn't like, of which he was, perhaps, also afraid. I felt the urge to run but was too frightened to move.

The soldiers obviously didn't find what they were looking for. I could see the angry disappointment in their faces. They were searching for something specific. I began to realize why they had come. Perhaps this sudden visit had something to do with those meetings with the boys—but how could it? No one had ever found out about the meetings, and we hadn't had any more. We had been collecting weapons and ammunition and hiding them, usually by burying them in private orchards, but that activity ended three months ago. Why would anyone be searching for those things now? We had also started to organize a small, underground print shop, for which I had stolen some printing type from the Soviet governmental print shop where I still worked as a pressman, but that activity had also been suspended temporarily. To be sure, a small, pedal-driven press was being assembled by another group unrelated to us, but I knew nothing about their activities now because none of the boys had contacted me for several weeks.

Although we had suspended our activities, it became obvious that the soldiers must be searching for the stolen font. Something must have happened to make me a suspect and bring these barbarians into our house. Now my thinking became clear: I must try to save the family! I couldn't get them involved in my clandestine activities.

The soldiers finished their search of the house. Two of them were already in the front vestibule, ready to leave, when one of them suddenly barked in a gruff military tone, "Don't you have an outside shed?"

There was a momentary silence. Then my old, frightened aunt answered very politely, "Yes, we do, sir, in back of the house."

Showing an air of self-assurance and arrogant authority, the soldiers turned immediately, without waiting to be led to the shed. My aunt was standing very close to me. When the soldier watching us momentarily relaxed his guard, I seized the opportunity and winked at my aunt to attract her attention. I gave her quick instructions, "It's under the sauerkraut barrel. Throw it out." She grasped the message immediately. I was not allowed to move from my spot, frozen by the threatening eyes of the guard aiming his rifle at me.

Aunt Frances told the guard that she would go and show the other two soldiers around. On the way out she stopped on the front porch, reached under the sauerkraut barrel, lifted the flat, heavy object wrapped in newspaper, and tossed it into the heap of snow piled outside the door. She then joined the two soldiers and proceeded to lead them to the animal shed. The soldiers found nothing suspicious, only my Angora rabbits in a cage and two piglets. Disappointed and swearing atrociously in Russian, the NKVD troopers returned to the kitchen. When they entered the kitchen, they remembered that they had not yet searched the front porch. They turned around and quickly searched the vestibule and enclosed porch, looking under the sauerkraut barrel at the last moment. As I saw the guard reaching under the sauerkraut barrel, I momentarily felt faint; I was scared, literally stiff, from fright, and angry at myself for bringing that stuff home. I was also angry at those brutal bastards for invading our home.

I was sweating all over and felt a terrible pressure to move my bowels, but that meant going to the outhouse. I did not know whether my dear aunt had had enough time to throw out the font. At first my aunt's face showed no clue, but then she gave me a fast, fleeting look full of good news. I almost fainted with relief. I had doubted that the old lady could lift the fairly heavy package, since it contained two pages of lead-alloy printing font.

The soldiers returned to the kitchen. By a series of quick, brutal shoves with their rifle butts, they separated me from the rest of the family and ordered me to go with them. The family thought in a silent, frozen panic, *Why do they want the boy? What will they do to him?*

But they could not question the soldiers. They knew that they would not get any answers. My aunt gathered up a set of clothes for me, but the guard stopped her. He said I didn't need any clothes—it would be enough for me to just put on a jacket over my nightclothes. I was to go to the militia station for identification and a few questions. He said I would be returned home within an hour. The soldiers would not even wait for me to tie my shoes. They were in a hurry to finish their job. I was too scared to show any emotion and just followed their orders. I had heard from some of my friends that their parents had been taken away some weeks or months earlier and never returned. These soldiers assured me that I would soon be home after answering a few questions.

Outside in Rogova Street a small, gray van waited for us. It was the middle of March 1940 and still wintry in the eastern Polish town of Lutsk. The snow lay on the ground, ten or twelve inches in most places, and fresh snow fell every few days. It was as if spring had been frightened off by all the horrible events happening in the country in recent months.

Two more soldiers were waiting in the van with submachine guns, just in case there was any resistance. One of them opened the back door and shoved me in. The vehicle started up quickly and began to move.

It was dark inside the van. Only a faint streak of light fell on the opposite wall. As I watched the line of light dance across the wall in front of me, I wondered why my aunt's family hadn't made more fuss or a greater protest at my being taken away. There was no doubt in my mind that they loved me. The only explanation that gave me solace was that the officer in charge had assured them I would be returned home soon. Besides, if they had protested too vigorously right then and there, it might have created an incident and led to the use of force and weapons by the soldiers. The family was helpless against soldiers with bayonets and submachine guns.

Things had changed very quickly in Lutsk over the past few months. It seemed that only yesterday I was a happy, carefree youth. As I rode in that dark van toward an uncertain fate, memories of a more pleasant time filled my thoughts. . . .

School Days

2

I have never stopped having nostalgic feelings about my youthful life in *Lutsk* (Polish name for Luck). Memories of those times have been like a spiritual fountain of strength and warmth to me in periods when the chilly winds of the Siberian winter were freezing the very marrow in my bones. It must be true what the ancient Romans believed, that in a healthy body there will be a healthy spirit. I also believe that the spirit of a person is more likely to carry on through life's ugly turns and maintain its viability, if in the formative young years it has been well nourished with wise love and a variety of constructive experiences.

My aunt's family was relatively poor, even judging by the generally low standards of those years between the two World Wars. We lived in the Volhynia province of Eastern Poland, which had been depopulated, neglected, and impoverished by more than a century-long and cruel tsarist Russian occupation. Many things like toys or sports equipment (e.g., bicycles, skates, skis, or toboggans) were unobtainable or much too expensive for a teenager from an average family.

Nonetheless, we managed to make the best of what we had, i.e., mainly our natural resources and our wits, to make our life happy and full of interesting activities for us youngbloods living in the Krasne suburb of Lutsk. In the summertime we often went to the public beach near the Krasne Bridge on the Styr River. We held competitions

The author in Poland (1939).

The author in Lutsk, Poland (1939).

At a railroad station in Baghdad, Iraq, en route to England (Spring 1943).

by the river in diving from the high banks into the clear water of the fast-flowing river below. We even dove from the bridge, which was treacherous because there were old pylons submerged underwater, invisible from above. Most of the youth, boys and girls, from Krasne and the neighboring villages, gathered on the beaches on both banks of the river.

Between sunbathing and swimming, we organized various games and contests to make the days go by faster. We played volleyball, soccer, leapfrog, and miscellaneous gymnastics, and showed off our trick-riding bicycle feats. I was finally able to buy myself a new bicycle when I started working in the bishopric printshop. After a great deal of practice, I was able to show off with a few unusual tricks, e.g., I could ride it standing on its seat (on one foot) or ride sitting on the handlebar.

In addition to these pastimes, we organized upstream boat trips on the Styr. For these trips we took only the bare necessities—matches, salt, bread, lard or salt pork, eating utensils, old metal army plates, and a frying pan and a pot or two for preparing our meals.

A long rope (about 150–200 feet in length) was also needed, since we usually hauled the boat twelve to fifteen miles upstream. The trip upstream took about two days. We took turns pulling the boat while one person sat in it, steering and rowing whenever there were deep inlets or the river was too winding. We took fishing poles, spare hooks, nets, and a container to hold the fish we caught, the staple of our meals while on the trip. White bass, smelt, and river perch were plentiful, in addition to the occasional slippery eel.

On the night before each trip, we had to find some bait for fishing. We could usually dig up some earthworms in our gardens. In addition to the worms, during the trip we visited farmhouses on either side of the river to catch flies.

The farmers, for the most part, welcomed us, because, first of all, we caused no damage to their properties. Second, they were glad to be getting free assistance in reducing the pesty population of flies in their farm sheds and in their own kitchens. They simply couldn't cope with these pests, which infested their cottages in the summer. We caught flies by the handful, squeezed their heads a little, and put them in a jar.

During our trek upstream we stopped every so often to rest, catch fish, and eat. We usually found a few potatoes or other vegetables in the fields to complement our diet.

At night we slept under the open skies, on the grass, or under a haystack. We had great fun recognizing the Big Dipper and other constellations or spotting shooting stars and making quick wishes. I had several secret wishes of my own, which I remember vaguely. I wanted to be a violinist and a scientist. I wanted to win the love of a cute girl who lived on a hill across the street from my aunt's house—her name was Helen Braun. But the dream that I cherished most while looking at the limitless expanse of the canopy studded with twinkling stars above us was to travel to the end of the world, to see mysterious places, and to witness the exotic wonders of faraway places. Sometimes I wasn't quick enough in specifying the whole "wish" that I wanted to come true. Then I felt sad, because right away I thought, *How can the stars get that wish for me if I don't tell them exactly what I want?*

In daytime the sun shone upon us, skylarks flew high and low, serenading the Creator, and graceful swallows tended their nests in the steeper parts of the riverbanks. It all seemed so beautiful, so much beauty of nature surrounding us everywhere, with all its wonders. It must have been God's country and we were close to Him then, because we certainly felt His peace and happiness.

Coming home took us about a third of the time of the journey upstream. Since the return trip was with the current, we could all ride in the boat, rowing where the current was too slow, or otherwise just steering and admiring the beautiful countryside beyond the banks of the river. We sang many of the songs that we learned in school or in scouts.

I belonged to a couple of youth organizations. The *Harcerstwo*, Boy Scouts, was one of these. We learned many practical skills—cooking, sewing, and many tricks for surviving in the wild. The special, close, personal relationships that existed among the boys in our boy-scout "family" unit taught us a great deal about cooperation with other people. The *Sokol*, Falcons, was another group that had a serious and far-reaching effect on me. It was a sports and gymnastics organization. Valdy, then my cousin Aleksandra's fiance, was an instructor of indoor and outdoor gymnastics, and he lured me into it. I loved the gymnasium hall they had and went there to practice once or twice a week. Even though I was relatively small in stature, I developed a strong and healthy body which served me very well through many difficult situations. Our motto in both the Boy Scouts and the Falcons was the Latin proverb *Mens sana, in corpore sano* (a healthy mind in a healthy body).

I was also an altar boy in the cathedral between the ages of ten and thirteen. That meant that I had to get up early in the morning and walk about five miles to serve mass. Learning the Latin responses for the mass didn't present much difficulty to me; I enjoyed serving at mass and singing Latin and Polish hymns. I also enjoyed many other church activities. On the Feast of Corpus Christi, we had very solemn processions marching through the streets of Lutsk. I always took part in marching, either as a boy scout or in a *Sokol* unit. At the age of twelve I started taking violin lessons and gave them a lot of attention. I enjoyed my lessons and willingly spent many additional hours on my own, learning to play Christmas carols and certain melodious songs popular at the time.

Even with all these activities, we still found time and energy for some not-so-innocent. youthful pranks. On top of a hill, just where Rogova Street branched off into a passage connecting it with Gorna Street, there was an ancient elm tree. Many people walked under that tree on their way to and from the city. We boys thought it would be fun to organize a way to annoy passing pedestrians. At night we would position ourselves in a bush some thirty to forty yards away and throw dirt up onto the tree. Of course, the pedestrians passing under the tree would immediately get angry upon feeling something fall on them. They would look up and threaten to "get us" up there. Really, they were shouting at an empty tree. Well, *we* thought it was funny.

Once five of us organized an exploratory trip to the secret underground tunnels of Count Lubart's thirteenth-century medieval castle. These tunnels, as we found out, connected the castle with the convent and cathedral next door. Since our preliminary investigations showed us that there was no light in the tunnels, we took a few candles and matches with us. The distance between the outer walls of the castle and the second and third basements of the cathedral was perhaps half a mile. We walked cautiously for about half an hour in this spooky tunnel, its floor littered with rocks, old bones, and, occasionally, a human skull staring at us from a ledge on the wall. Those were the remains of people who had taken part in the several wars, battles, and uprisings that had been fought in those lands. Their bodies had been hidden, abandoned, disintegrated, or eaten away by rodents. We had to clear away giant cobwebs stretched out in weird patterns across the tunnel. It must have taken a lot of time for those huge spiders, the artisans of the dark, to weave their nets, and they angrily scuttled out of our way. I often wondered how such little creatures could produce, in complete darkness, such artfully designed masterpieces of nets, stretching across the entire tunnel, measuring about seven to eight feet from the floor to the ceiling and the same in width. It has been a great mystery to me ever since!

We were all scared, but not one of us would admit it. We each held our candle forward and walked "bravely" on, keeping a pretty tight formation. Stories were told that the souls of the medieval heroes lived in those tunnels while serving their penance—it was their purgatory before they could be admitted into the Land of the Eternal Peace. Suddenly we heard a faint, high-pitched shriek as a bat streaked past us. A couple of rats, scared by us, ran across our path, awakening all the sleeping spiders who scuttled away angrily after giving us some threatening looks. They disappeared into the webbed darkness before we could see them clearly. As the spiders glided into their holes, we tightened our single-file formation, holding closely behind each other. We all felt cold fright shivers going through us, though no one would dare admit it. Every so often we made the sign of the cross in order to keep the evil spirits at a safe distance from us.

Then the tunnel took a turn and we didn't feel like pursuing its course any farther. However, we noticed an opening about eight to ten feet above the floor. Of course we had to examine it, so the group raised me up onto its shoulders.

When my candle spread its faint, flickering rays through the murky space in front of me, I saw shelves upon shelves of pigeonholes filled with bottles. I reported my discovery down to the leader of the expedition, "It looks like a wine cellar!"

That's precisely what it was. My fellow pirates ordered me to pass a bottle to them for inspection. When they read the label on the bottle, their decision was quick and unanimous: "Pass down three bottles." Then they lowered me down and we traced our way back to the entrance under the castle. We hurried back to our own territory on the large meadow near my house, where we opened two bottles right away and each had two or three good gulps. Yes, it was a well-aged, vintage cathedral wine, and we were a happy, drunken, singing group of boys that night.

The winter seasons brought many other happy adventures. There was a large frozen meadow nearby, approximately three to four miles in diameter, that we used for skating. This marshy meadow was usually flooded by the autumn rains. Besides ordinary skating, we organized races and stunt competitions. Ice racing was done by using hand-held sails; sometimes it was an open winter coat held up to the wind. The wind in the open meadow blew powerfully, and gusts would occasionally propel a skater for long distances, at speeds far exceeding those an average foot skater is capable of.

There were hills nearby for skiing and tobogganing. Because my friends and I weren't rich enough to buy professionally made winter sports equipment, we devised methods to manufacture our own skates, toboggans, and skis. The skates were made from two little boards of ashwood, one being on top, in a flat horizontal position, and the other attached to the bottom of the first one by its side. To the bottom board we affixed a piece of wire, the latter being square in its cross-section. The bottom side of the wire had to be filed off to make a sharp edge, needed to cut the ice while skating. Skis were easily made of ashwood boards, bent and shaped using a steam kettle. Toboggans were also easy to make from the same kind of wood. To make the runners smoother, we affixed metal strips to the bottom side. These toboggans were as fast and efficient as their factory made counterparts. Admittedly, they weren't painted or varnished to a high polish, and they weren't quite as elegant as the store-bought ones, but we loved them and were proud of them.

We even managed to attach ourselves, on toboggans or skis, to the rear end of a bus on one of the main streets in town. We were pulled by the bus for a mile or so. Occasionally there were bad spills, but I don't remember any serious injuries resulting from them.

Once some geniuses from our group thought of a way to introduce more variety and excitement to our ice arena. They drove a thick pole into the bottom of the icy lake. When it seemed well frozen they took a long bar of timber, about twenty-five to thirty feet in length, and attached one end of it to the pole with a leather loop in such a way that the bar could be turned around the pole. A number of boys would hold onto the bar and skate faster and faster, around and around, picking up speed and centrifugal force. Eventually the skaters could not hold on any more and would let go of the bar, fall on their behinds, and slide away on the ice.

We had a lot of fun with this contraption until one day I happened to be the one on the far end of the bar. The whirling reached such a high speed that I couldn't hold on any longer. The whiplash effect was so powerful that I was thrown far away from the pole, in the direction of a marshy area where the ice was pretty thin. I couldn't control the direction of my sliding or my speed. I couldn't stop myself from sliding onto the thin ice. The ice broke under me and I went down into about six feet of frigid water. I tried to get out, but the ice kept collapsing under my flailing arms. I frantically held onto the floating ice chunks, bobbing up and down. Assistance was difficult to organize because no one could get close enough to pull me out. Eventually, however, someone detached the long bar from the pole and extended it out to me. I grabbed it with all the waning force in my numbed hands, and after one or two attempts, the boys managed to pull me on top of the ice and away from the hole. Several boys covered me with their coats and rushed me home.

My aunt Frances was mortified when she saw my limp, convulsing body being brought into the house. She wasted no time, however, and heated some bricks in the hot baking oven. She stripped me naked, dried me, and put warm clothes on me. I was put in bed under heavy covers, with hot bricks wrapped in rags on both sides of me. It was not meant to be my final hour, for two days later, I was out playing again. It was a lucky ending to something that could have ended in tragedy. All in all, I think Aunt Frances shed more tears and went through more anguish than I suffered. It was an example of the resiliency of youth.

My aunt Frances had cared for me since I was three, when my mother died leaving me the youngest of four sons and a daughter. My father was never much interested in his offspring and, when left alone to care for a brood of five, decided that since God gave him these children, God would take care of them somehow. And omniscient God wasted no time in arranging my life—when Aunt

Frances went to her sister's funeral in Warsaw, she didn't hesitate about taking the little three-year-old, snow–white–haired orphan, Richard. We were considered orphaned because no one in the family thought that our father could or would want to take care of us. My mother's brother John lived next door to Aunt Frances in Lutsk. He also attended the funeral in Warsaw, and returned home with my sister, Maria, who was about three years older than I. Both of us were separated by some two hundred miles from our remaining three brothers, who were later adopted (unofficially) by various relatives.

I never had a reason to feel homesick for Warsaw. I was adopted into a family of four children, and soon became the baby of my new family. My aunt Frances was a woman richly endowed with the qualities that matter most in life—human compassion, generosity, love, and goodwill towards people, and a kind disposition. She and her husband went to the south of Russia before World War I in seach of employment, since economic conditions for Poles in Tsarist Poland were very difficult. Through her experiences, she developed a poor woman's healthy sense for survival. Although she herself was an illiterate woman without many worldly goods or much income, she had acquired an uncanny wisdom for guiding a family towards gainful adult careers.

Aunt Frances was the main breadwinner of the family. She worked as a helper to a dentist in the downtown section of Lutsk. Her husband's only talent that I knew of was dodging real work. He was a man without any definable trade or ambition, who was also inclined to drink. Since vodka and all flavored alcoholic beverages were relatively expensive, he drank blue-dyed denatured alcohol. This was, supposedly, a deadly poison to most normal people, but Uncle Hieronim lived quite a contented life until the age of eighty, despite his unusual tastes in drinking. He died in the early 1980s.

Aunt Frances and Uncle Hieronim had two sons and two daughters. The eldest, Mietek, was in his thirties. He had put himself through accounting school and was married and on his own. He didn't have much to do with me since I was just a small boy. I remember meeting him and his wife, Niusia, on certain occasions. They were rather indifferent toward me.

Next in age were the two daughters, Hanna and Aleksandra. Both completed elementary education, followed by a two-year program of courses in homemaking, primarily sewing and cooking.

The youngest child was named Chester (Czeslaw). He was like a real brother to me. He was my protector and my advisor, being all of five years my elder. We had complete trust in each other. When he wanted to play hooky, I covered for him, both in school and at home. We would leave the house together at the usual time in the morning to walk to School No. 4. Chester had a passion for soccer. A block away from the house he would just take off and go his own way, to join his friends on the soccer practice field near the Styr River. I would tell the school principal, Chester's homeroom teacher, and other teachers, if asked, that Chester was sick at home. At about 3:30 P.M. Chester would meet me at the same spot where he left me that morning. At home, Aunt Frances would ask us how our day went at school. We usually synchronized our stories in advance, after I briefed him on the day's events, and he seldom, if ever, got into trouble for missing school. In return for my cooperation, Chester allowed me to tag along on trips to the forest, or on the boat trips that were organized by his older group of friends.

I was not much interested in playing soccer, although

I went to see the games once in a while. For us, the younger set, playing volleyball or tennis was more fun. I learned to play tennis fairly well while working at the tennis court, picking up balls for the adult players. This part-time job in the afternoons and Saturdays earned me sufficient spending money for movies. Among my favorite movies were American Western cowboy stories, such as Tom Mix movies, Hopalong Cassidy, and *The Last of the Mohicans*, or sea voyages, e.g., J. Conrad's *Lord Jim*, and others.

The school years went by in an atmosphere of full acceptance and affection in my adopted home. I saw my real sister, Maria, frequently, and she treated me with sisterly love and concern. She often included me in her social activities. When she invited her school friends for parties at her thatch-roofed home, she also invited me. She and her girl friends taught me to dance when I was between twelve and fourteen years old. I became quite good at the tango, slow waltz, fast waltz, and foxtrot. We used an RCA record player that had to be wound by hand. It had a big horn on it and a label with a picture of a dog, and a sign saying HIS MASTER'S VOICE.

I enjoyed being a student in the two elementary schools I attended. I liked my teachers and my grades were good. Language arts was my favorite subject. For the first two grades my aunt registered me in School No. 2, located within the walls of Count Lubart's castle. It was one of the more reputable schools in town, attended mostly by children of families who were either descendants of the ancient Polish families from the eastern areas of Poland who had survived the ravages and persecutions of the 123-year Tsarist Russian occupation, or people who had been relocated from central Poland by the Polish government shortly after World War I. The latter were referred to, unfairly, as "colonists."

I had to walk about six miles to school. In the warm months it was fun. However, in the frosty winter months, chilly northeastern winds blew unabated across the Russian plains from the White Sea and the Ural Mountains. It was deathly cold for young students walking across the Krasne Bridge and the wide-open spaces near the frozen river. There were several incidents of near-drowning when boys tried to take shortcuts across the Styr River. In many places the water just barely froze because of the whirling, fast eddy currents below.

In the third grade I was transferred to a local school in our neighborhood, No. 4. This school was predominantly populated by local ethnic children, many from nearby villages, mostly Ukrainians, but also Czechoslovaks, Jews, and White Russians whose parents had escaped from the Communist Revolution of 1917. Native Polish children were in the minority.

I soon made friends among the students of the various ethnic minorities. Before long, I discovered my natural ability to assimilate their respective languages and also some of their customs, which made it much easier to communicate with the multilingual youngsters. By speaking with them I learned to accept their cultural values and attitudes and to understand them on an intimate level.

In time, I also became the arbiter of many disputes, verbal as well as physical feuds between the local ethnic students (mostly Ukrainian boys) and the children of the Polish families from Central Poland, who had been encouraged by the interwar Polish government to resettle in the eastern regions of the country in order to "re-Polonize" these areas. The Russians, during their 123-year long occupation of those lands, had systematically reduced the native Polish population in the occupied territory, by resettling the Poles to the east, into the vast territories inside

Russia proper (European and Asian parts). The children of these recent incoming settlers, for the most part, did not consider it gratifying or necessary to learn the strange local languages. I, on the other hand, was rewarded for cultivating these friendships by being invited into the homes of these children, in the city as well as in the surrounding villages.

From the time I first learned to read, I was an avid reader. In my early teens I read virtually everything I came across, but I was particularly interested in stories from other countries. At one time, I remember, I was thrilled by the stories and legends of the American Wild West. My heroes included Tom Mix, from several American Westerns and Uncle Tom, from *Uncle Tom's Cabin*. I also dreamt of going down the Mississippi River on a raft with Huck Finn. My boat trips on the Styr River were just like the adventures of Tom Sawyer and Huckleberry Finn. Another thriller was Defoe's *Robinson Crusoe*, which had a strong appeal to my youthful fancy. These books were, of course, in Polish translations. My favorite books by native Polish authors included Henryk Sienkiewicz's *In the Desert and Wilderness*, a beautiful story of two young children, a Polish boy, Stas, and an English girl, Nelly, caught in an unscheduled, dangerous African safari; the historical trilogy, from the sixteenth and seventeenth centuries, consisting of *The Deluge, With the Sword and Fire,* and *Pan Wolodyjowski*, and a novel about the life of the first Christians in Rome in the time of Julius Caesar, *Quo Vadis*.

The school principal, Mr. Red'ko, a Ukrainian, knew me quite well for my academic achievements and also for the frequent feuds and fights in which I was involved. Mr. Red'ko liked me and was always very fair in meting out punishments for these forbidden altercations. My aunt Frances was asked many times to come to see the principal on my behalf, most often to explain my involvement in these feuds, even though other students were usually implicated as well.

Mr. Red'ko and my teachers recommended that my aunt seek a scholarship for my further education, but her requests were turned down. My aunt's next decision was to make a tradesman out of me. One of our neighbors, Mr. Oskierko, worked in the diocesan printing shop. Through good luck, plus his good word on my behalf, I was accepted as an apprentice to a pressman at the print shop in the bishop's headquarters. I was to learn the pressman's trade, which seemed to me a fair and intellectually stimulating trade at the ripe old age of fourteen.

By the age of fifteen I was promoted to a full journeyman printer. Bosses and customers praised my work and told me that I was the youngest pressman they had known in the business. But the pride, self-satisfaction, and good wages didn't last very long. In the summer months, articles appeared in the newspapers about the German claims concerning the "Polish Corridor," the narrow strip of land on the Pomerania given to Poland in the peace treaty of 1918. It allowed Poland access to the Baltic Sea. Various clients and visitors coming to my machine room nervously talked about the political tension in Europe. Toward the end of the summer of 1939, after many political maneuvers between von Ribbentrop of the Third Reich and Molotov of the USSR, the tremors of war could be felt with increasing intensity throughout all of Europe.

The Outbreak of War

3

For months prior to September 1939, tension in Central Europe grew daily. The Polish government, under Ignacy Moscicki, set in motion a general mobilization of military forces. All young males between the ages of eighteen and twenty-five were drafted into military service. Young Germans with Polish citizenship, who were eligible for conscription in the military, escaped by the hundreds across the border into German-controlled Prussia. Germans living in the central and western sections of Poland were instructed by Nazi agents to organize a resistance against the mobilization in the form of public rallies and marches. In the industrial city of Lodz, sometimes called the Polish Manchester because of its vastly developed textile industry, mass demonstrations and work strikes were organized among women factory workers by Nazi agents. Posters carried by the demonstrators denounced the mobilization of military forces as being provocative and inflammatory because a ten-year pact of nonaggression had just been signed by the German foreign minister von Ribbentrop and his Polish counterpart, Minister Jozef Beck. The chief of the German government mass propaganda was Paul Joseph Goebbels, known as the "Master of Deceit," Goebbels's world-scale lies were planned years ahead of time.

This Goebbels-inspired Nazi propaganda was primarily to lull the Polish nation and government into a blissful state of unpreparedness. The Germans had been planning a military attack for many years and wanted to prevent the Polish government from having well-trained and well-armed military forces. Suddenly, with some falsified provocations, and no declaration of war, the motorized Nazi panzer divisions made synchronized attacks on all border posts along Poland's western border. They simply drove their steel formations through the border gates, crushing the Polish national eagle emblems under their wheels. The tanks rolled, unchallenged, past the nonaggression pact posters that still hung from buildings and electrical poles throughout Poland.

Poland's military equipment was outdated and in short supply. The physical condition and the state of battle preparedness of the Polish military forces were badly lagging in numbers and in modern efficiency. Even the country's border posts were, in many cases, poorly protected, undermanned, and ill-equipped with modern weapons. There were many examples of undaunted heroism among the units of the Polish border defense corps, such as the defense of the Westerplatte outpost near Gdansk (formerly Danzig). In other cases, the Polish cavalry formations put up a brave front and charged with swords and single-shot rifles against the modern German panzer divisions, with devastating results for the cavalrymen and their horses.

For many months before the Nazi invasion of Poland, the Soviet Red Army prepared for a simultaneous attack on Poland's eastern frontier. Even before Soviet military forces mobilized their divisions along the Polish border, NKVD agents had enlisted great numbers of sympathetic agitators inside Poland. These collaborators were called the "fifth column," and were responsible for many diversionary tactics that were executed throughout the easternmost Polish provinces. These collaborators were paid in rubles or gold for their work, or were promised high positions in the future Poland, when the People's party would be in power.

It was therefore no coincidence that the same agents and agitators who appeared at various public antigovernment rallies before the war were also seen working together with the Red Army in high administrative and leadership positions. These individuals spread the Soviet propaganda that the Red Army was the great liberator and defender of the Polish people against the atrocities of Nazi Germany. Wherever there was any sporadic resistance mobilized against the Bolshevik tanks, or any anti-Soviet sabotage, it was countered and denounced by these brigades of spies and collaborators. Thus, the Red Army met with only slight resistance while overrunning the eastern half of Poland.

Just seven years prior to this, in 1932, the Soviets had signed a mutual-assistance agreement with the Polish government against German aggression. On August 23, 1939, foreign ministers of Nazi Germany and the USSR signed a secret pact for the Fourth Partition of Poland. One week after this pact was signed, on September 1, 1939, German Luftwaffe bombers struck all major Polish cities, particularly military and other strategic sites, with thousands of tons of devastating explosives and incendiary bombs.

The people of the town of Lutsk first heard the frightening, soul-destroying whines of air raid sirens on the morning of Saturday, September 2, 1939.

I was just on my way to work in the diocesan print shop in order to finish running a religious monthly periodical. Halfway across the Kosciuszko Bridge, which connected the suburb of Krasne with the main section of the city, I stopped because of the warning air raid sirens. The sirens wailed so loudly that it was impossible not to react to their noise. At the same time, I heard a strange voice from within me, telling me plainly not to go to the print shop, but return home. The voice was so friendly and convincing that I turned around and quickly went home. By then there was an oppressive excitement in the air, so I passed by my aunt's house and headed for Uncle John's fruit orchard, feeling somewhat disappointed at not being able to finish the printing order.

The day was sunny, and visibility was perfect. The skies were only sparsely dotted with fluffy, snow-white clouds, suspended from a high ceiling of blue. A few minutes passed and I began to hear the low-pitched hum of several dozen aircraft engines. In threes, like cranes migrating to their winter habitats, bombers with German Luftwaffe markings approached the city from the southwest.

I flung myself on the grass under a plum tree, where the ground sloped down toward the creek and a marshy meadow. The creek was almost entirely dried up, since there hadn't been much rainfall that summer. Even as I watched the bombers approaching overhead, I did not realize what hell was about to fall upon our town. I soon noticed that a few planes began to make a shallow dip, and then dive, breaking away from the rest of the group. As they dove they released bombs while still flying in perfect unison.

The first bombs were dropped on the bishop's quarters. Almost immediately smoke rose in huge clouds. The bombers continued on their bombing mission. The formations that followed were now scattered, bombing different parts of the city. It looked as if it was all nicely planned and rehearsed, or as if the whole operation were expertly guided by someone who had a perfect view over the whole area and was directing the whole action. A few formations targeted the provincial capital headquarters, others went over to the railway station, and the remaining trios split themselves neatly between the military barracks and the local airport, dropping their deadly packages everywhere. The city was covered in smoke now, and the air raid sirens wailed their desperate warnings.

Lying down on the sloping hill, I had a perfect view over the entire meadow, all the way across to the far side of it, where the Ukrainian villages of Hnidava and Polonka were located.

In less than an hour the enemy bombers had fulfilled their murderous mission and quickly disappeared in the direction from which they came. There was no opposition, and no antiaircaft shots were fired on that day. The surprise had been complete.

The harvest of death and destruction was shattering. Everyone was momentarily paralyzed by the shock. Soon after the planes disappeared in the direction of Czechoslovakia, where they were stationed, many people started toward the central sections of the city, where most of the bombs had struck.

I went with a group of people across the Styr River, but I was mainly concerned with the results of the bombing of the bishopric, specifically the printing house establishment. I ran to see for myself what damage had resulted. As I approached the grounds of the bishopric, I saw from a distance that the main building of the bishop's headquarters had suffered a direct hit. But I still hoped that the print shop may have been missed. Almost the entire front of the building was destroyed, particularly near the entrance. Bodies were strewn on the front lawn, some of them literally torn apart, with limbs or heads severed from their bodies. At first I was horrified, stunned, and felt sick to my stomach, but the tragic urgency of the moment pushed me on. There was general pandemonium and confusion. The smell of death was everywhere. The wounded were carried into undamaged parts of the building, where the doctors and nurses had already started giving them first aid. Later they were to be taken to hospitals, though few were still in serviceable condition.

Walking toward the side of the large building complex where the print shop was located, I saw that the damage on this end of the building was minor, at least from what could be seen on the outside. The people who lived in this part of the building, above the print shop, were all members of the bishop's staff—two families of servants and caretakers of the grounds. They had taken cover in the basement when the air raid sirens had sounded. Now they came out of the basement, shocked, crying and shaking, but physically unharmed.

The only real damage in this part of the building complex was where one stray bomb had hit the roof, tearing a huge hole in the ceiling and floor of the apartment. My heart stopped its quick thumping and my insides went cold as I entered the shop. Huge chunks of concrete covered the floor. Directly above the new, modern printing press (made in Dresden, Germany) was a large hole, which let in a bright shaft of sunlight.

An unexploded German bomb lay on the flatbed of the machine on which I had worked only the day before. I felt a queasy emptiness when I realized that I could have been buried under this rubble if I had come to work that morning. I couldn't help thinking that the Lord Almighty must have wanted me spared that day. It was His voice that whispered to me to turn back and not go to work in the morning. I felt dizzy and as if my legs were about to fold under me, as I stood there momentarily, watching people milling around, to and fro, most of them crying in desperation. But why were so many innocent people to be hurt and killed?

I didn't have much time to dwell on the reasons for all the tragedy around me. There was too much chaos and commotion outside. People were crying and running about, taking care of all the casualties lying around the main part of the building. I made the sign of the cross in thanksgiving, and quickly joined in to offer help where needed.

Stories were being told about the terrible destruction in other parts of the city, and about the many deaths caused either directly by the bombs or indirectly by fires or collapsing buildings. Some people had been running through the streets during the air raid and were killed when they were thrown against buildings by the impact of an air blast from the exploding bombs.

The provincial headquarters was virtually demolished, with many casualties. The railway station was hit by several bombs. Those must have been some powerful bombs, because even the railway carriages were turned upside down. Trains, as well as buildings, were destroyed. At the airport the standing planes were either destroyed immediately or set on fire by the exploding incendiary bombs. Many cities throughout Poland were as exposed and unprotected as ours, since war had not been officially declared. We experienced firsthand the element of surprise that was an important part of the modern blitzkrieg warfare used by the Nazis.

As the German front line pushed eastward, people collected their possessions in sacks or on horsedrawn wagons and fled via the highways. The German planes flew very low over the countryside, machine-gunning civilians on the highways who were fleeing in panic from their homes. They were easy targets for the German bombers.

Some people had cars and, of course, they put their possessions in and on top of the cars—but when they ran out of gasoline, they had to abandon the cars, with all the contents, right in the middle of the road, thus causing complete traffic jams.

When the German bombings stopped, the Soviet Red Army invaded Poland from the East, as if it had been prearranged.

September 17, 1939, was a clear day. The Russian tanks arrived that day in Lutsk. From early morning there was much excitement in the streets. Crowds of people were lining up in the streets. The news was out—the Russians were coming! I also went out to see them. I went to Jagiellonska Street in the early afternoon. I saw the huge, dusty tanks thudding heavily on the newly laid hexagonal pavement. They came from the southeast. The turret hatches were open and the gunmen were visible, standing and watching the crowd in the street. The crowd stood quietly, passively, and unenthusiastically. If there were any angry people in the crowd, they were quiet.

As the tanks approached the place where I was standing, I noticed there were flowers lying on the tops of some tanks. There were also placards on the fronts of some tanks, saying: "Welcome, the Mighty Red Army!" A few zealots were walking along beside the tanks, looking joyful, even triumphant. They wore red armbands. For some, it was love at first sight. But the news started going around that some policemen, public officials, and others who were involved in the public offices, schools, and related services were being sought out. Many were arrested the first day, more disappeared the next day, and the next, and every day after that. The gray van of the NKVD cruised through the streets, mostly at night.

The Soviets brought ready-made plans for purging

Polish society, all agreed upon in secret talks between Hitler and Stalin, and their foreign ministers. Both partners were to enforce a policy to destroy the Polish intellectual elite, political and business leadership, as well as the lowest levels of organized national and social life. Mass murder and deportation of millions were their tools. In order to achieve that goal, a semblance of normal life had to be reestablished. That way the new authorities would know better where everybody lived and what positions various individuals occupied in the social hierarchy.

The Bolsheviks soon established an almost normal life in the town. The stores reopened, even though they had no new food supplies. The Red Army ordered the school administrators—that is, the few who had not been carted off to prisons—to open the schools. By a special *ukaz* (public notice), they urged parents to send their children to school. Of course, the Bolsheviks wanted to have the children in school so that they could exercise better, closer control over them, and thereby exercising a better control of the whereabouts of their parents, who before long were to be relocated, i.e., shipped to the resettlement camps in Siberia.

In school we had to attend many propaganda meetings. At these meetings the Communist political commissars told us that the old, traditional system of thinking had collapsed and that the teachings of Marx, Engels, and Lenin pointed to a new direction for future generations. A new life was going to be built, based on practical applications of modern scientific discoveries. Various religions, the commissar told us, were nothing but the opium used by the priests and the bourgeoisie system to hold back the vast majority of people, in order to exploit them. Some of this talk made us think, for a moment, that perhaps there was something good for us in this new order.

In their speeches the *politruks* (political leaders, commissars) pointed out that those in the poor working class really had nothing going for them in the capitalist system. Indeed, we could see that Poland was largely poor. The ravages and neglect of the tsarist Russian, German (Prussian), and Austrian occupations prior to World War I, and the destruction of World War I military operations of various kinds, had left Poland in shambles. There was widespread unemployment and poverty. Even a secondary education was unattainable for the children of the vast underprivileged social class. What the politruks told us about our plight was true—we could see it ourselves. Of course, they didn't tell us that social conditions for the general masses of ordinary people in the Soviet Union since the Revolution of 1917, were a thousand times worse. We were soon to find out about those things.

Even though we accepted and agreed with some parts of what the politruks told us, we did not want to discard the freedoms we enjoyed. Our religious and social traditions, our proud national history was all a part of us, and we a part of it. We asked many questions, too many, at these political meetings, and the political commissars were furious because they could not convince us.

In order to secularize the schools and, by the same action, to lessen the influence and the control the church had upon us all, the authorities ordered a new school attendance schedule. Up to that time we had a six-day school week and the seventh, Sunday, was the day of rest, except for the obligation to attend the holy mass at the church. The Soviet authorities would not accept that system—they wanted to pull us away from the church and religion. We were to have a six-day school week, with the seventh day off. However, Sunday would no longer be a holiday.

Our new teachers had many new things to tell us. A new star ("red," we added quietly) had risen for mankind, they told us, and it pointed to new directions for all people. All this talk and the new theories were largely unacceptable to the Christian students. The first Sunday on which we were supposed to attend school, the Christian students boycotted their classes and went to church instead. After about six weeks of booing, laughing, and shouting and occasional tomato and egg throwing during meetings, the Soviet commissars ordered the schools closed. When the schools closed we were disappointed and embittered. There were no jobs, and life was full of general confusion. The future looked very grim, uncertain, and full of danger. A group of us Polish students began to meet privately in small groups to discuss current events and the general situation in the country. It was the nucleus of our future organization. We met in different places so as not to arouse the suspicions of the Soviet secret police. We were dedicated young people, with deeply ingrained patriotic convictions. We knew of the many arrests being made day and night. Many of our parents were taken away, never to return.

Polish soldiers were retreating from the western front, their military units defeated and scattered. Some soldiers hid their weapons, hoping to have use for them some time later, should the fortunes of war take a different turn. Others just tossed their weapons and ammunition anywhere—in the bushes or in the ditches by the roadside—and changed into civilian clothes in a hurry, so that they wouldn't be caught in uniform by the Soviets or their agents. If a man was caught in any uniform, whether it was military, police, border defense corps, or even a boyscout uniform, he was, in most cases, either shot on the spot before there was time for any questions to be asked or else "interned," which meant he was immediately shipped to a Soviet prison or prison camp. By the winter of 1939–40, it became increasingly obvious that that phase of the war had run its course. Throughout that period of time, we teenagers came across a lot of hidden weapons of various kinds, and many boxes of ammunition.

We planned various activities for the future. Each member was assigned a specific area of activity, the success of which was primarily his responsibility. My specific assignment was to obtain printing equipment and supplies, including printing fonts and paper, if at all possible. This would be a good start toward a small print shop, until we could gain access to more substantial equipment. The material was to be used to print pamphlets and communiques for Polish resistance groups. I managed to get a job in the local Soviet government printing house because of my previous work experience in the diocesan printing shop. Working in the government printing house, I had access to printing fonts. I took several packets of font and hid them properly—all but the last packet, the one under the sauerkraut barrel.

My adoptive family knew nothing of my recent activities outside the home, so I was particularly elated and grateful that no evidence was found during the search of our house. I decided, of course, to plead not guilty to anything with which I might be charged, for I was sure that the NKVD had neither proof nor witnesses against me. My aunt's family would also be safe because no incriminating evidence was found in the house. They could plead innocence and be spared any recriminations.

Interrogations Begin

4

After the police van had made several turns, I sensed instinctively that we were not going to the local militia station. Through the little cracks in the rear door I could tell that I was being taken across the Kosciuszko Bridge to the central part of the city. I caught glimpses of the Jagiellonska Street and the cathedral. Shortly after we passed Count Lubart's castle the police van stopped.

I heard a heavy, squeaking gate being opened. When the door of the wagon opened, the first thing I saw was the bayonet of the guard's rifle. Behind the rifle stood a Mongolian face—coldly expressionless, threatening, and ready to shoot if I made a wrong move.

I was inside the massive prison walls, where many unpleasant surprises awaited me. Many hopes and innocent, naive expectations were killed the first day. A cold shiver went through me. So! The guards and their leader had lied to my family. They didn't bring me to a police station for an identification. This is the prison!

"Vihodi! [Come out]" the guard shouted. I obeyed the order quickly and silently. I was marched to the prison receiving room with one guard in front of me and one behind, both armed with bayonetted rifles, and an additional guard a few steps behind us, armed with a submachine gun.

They led me under heavy guard, as if I were the world's meanest criminal. My nerves were taut, like the strings of a well-tuned violin, where the slightest touch produces powerful sound. I heard the fast beating of my heart, and my temples were pulsating so hard that I was sure the guards would notice it.

In the receiving room I was told to turn around and face the wall, and then I was searched. All loose articles, such as a strap I had around my pajamas, the contents of my pockets, and even my shoelaces were taken, and everything was deposited in a pigeonhole. I didn't have any valuables on me. I was ordered to sign the list and was told that I would get the articles back when I was released. (Another lie! I never saw any of those things again.) I was led into another room, where a prison barber shaved my head close to the scalp with hair clippers. At that moment my hopes of getting out of there anytime soon were dashed. I was solidly within the prison walls.

I was led through the prison corridors by a guard holding a large ring of keys walking silently in front of me, another armed guard behind me. Twice during the twenty-minute walk I was stopped suddenly and ordered to turn around and face the wall. As we stood still, I heard the steps of another team of guards leading a prisoner from the opposite direction. Evidently this was the established routine. The idea was that the prisoners must not see each other, since mutual recognition might lead to outside leaks of information about those in prison, which might be of value to the resistance movement. Even though the corridors were dimly lit throughout the entire five-hundred-year-old prison complex, every effort was made to prevent prisoners from recognizing one another.

I was brought into a cell no more than fifteen feet by fifteen feet, with a dim bulb above the entrance. At first I could see nothing. As my eyes began to adjust to the darkness, I gradually made out several heads raised from the floor, where fifteen to twenty men were sleeping. I stood near the door because I couldn't see any empty place on the floor to sit or lie down.

I was in shock for a long time after the guard turned the heavy key in the door behind me. As I became accustomed to the darkness of the room, I recognized three or four fathers of my former playmates, all of whom had been policemen in my neighborhood.

One or two unshaven, dirty faces recognized me as well and started waving their hands to me, motioning for me to come closer. They appeared to be a very sad and miserable lot. I just stood there, even after my eyes had adjusted to the darkness. I was paralyzed by the sight of so many desperately helpless human beings. They looked like the damned sinners in Dante's *Divine Comedy*, condemned to perpetual suffering in the semidarkness of Hades, without any hope of ever being redeemed. I stood there in a psychic shock, too scared to move. I found it very difficult to realize fully what a tremendous sudden change had come about in my life. In spite of this obvious tragedy, I still had no idea of what my present plight had become.

The men lying on the floor were raising their heads one after another and looked at me in curious disbelief. In whispers, they asked me how and why I got myself into prison. They were anxious to heard the news from the outside. Some of them had been in the prison, even the same cell, for as long as twelve weeks. They knew nothing of the latest developments in the war or occupation activities. None of them knew why they were being held captive or what fate the NKVD captors were preparing for them. Most had been taken out to the NKVD posts for "identification and a few questions."

They had been asked many personal as well as general

questions. The NKVD agents wanted to know all about the members of their families and the names of their friends, co-workers, and neighbors. Soon after any new names were mentioned, new people were brought into the prison. Orders for new people to be hunted and brought into captivity were issued even before an interrogation ended, before the person under investigation himself was returned to his prison cell. Prisoners being questioned soon learned not to give anyone's name or whereabouts, to spare others from being brought into the same torturous treatment.

After standing there silently for a few minutes, I moved forward with great effort through the half-sleeping bodies of men, to the place where the two men with faces familiar to me were inviting me.

One of them asked me in a whisper, "What's your name? I remember your face well!"

"Richard," I answered quietly, still in a shock, not fully comprehending my situation, and, of course, more scared by the minute.

"Why did they bring you here?" the other man asked.

"I don't know."

They all looked sad and miserable, their yellow-gray faces pictures of complete hopeless resignation. Their eyes had lost the sparkle of life and happiness. We talked in whispers because compulsory silence was enforced. They asked many questions, since they were hungry for news about their families, about the war, and about the world at large. I told them what I knew about their loved ones, about new arrests, and of people disappearing quite often, never to be seen again.

I spent at least two weeks in that cell, not knowing the charges against me. One day the messenger guard, the harbinger of doom, as we called him, came into the cell and called out. "Is there anybody whose last name starts with an *L*?" I answered with my name and he said, "Come with me, and be quick."

My first trip to the NKVD investigative headquarters held several surprises for me. I was barely sixteen, a pale-faced boy of rather small stature, weighing less than one hundred pounds, and generally sickly in appearance. I didn't have the threatening look of being a counterrevolutionary soldier, the charge with which I was soon to be labeled.

When I was brought into the interrogator's office, he wasn't there yet. The guard told me to sit down at the front of the desk so I would be facing the interrogator when he sat in his chair. My first interrogator was a young lieutenant in his mid-twenties, tall and handsome, with light blond hair. He seemed in a good mood and started his business right away.

"Your name is Risha'rd Julianovich L., is that right?"

"Yes," I said.

"I am going to be your interrogator. My name is Lieutenant Kuznetzov. We may not have to meet many times if you cooperate by immediately telling me the whole truth about yourself and all your activities. Then you will be allowed to go home. So let's begin. What were you arrested for?"

"I don't know, citizen investigator," I answered.

It was the truth. I didn't know for which of my activities I was arrested, nor did I know how much information the NKVD had compiled on me. My first answer didn't please the interrogator.

"Now, I don't want to hear that kind of an answer!" he burst out in anger. "Do you understand me? I want the truth."

"That is the truth," I replied.

He pounded on the desktop furiously with his fist. "Tell me the truth before I get angry with you!" he shouted. "You must tell me more about yourself, your past life, and about your friends and relatives. What organizations did you belong to?" Kuznetzov fired questions at me in rapid succession, all the while looking intently into my face.

"I belonged to the boy scouts and the Sokols," I answered. Then I added, "Oh, I also served God at the church."

"We'll talk about your god and your church later," he said offhandedly. "Now tell me about the boy scouts and the Sokols. Did you believe in them?"

"Yes, I believed in what we were doing. I always enjoyed our activities. We listened to lectures and we went on trips and campouts. I learned a lot every time we met."

"What were the lectures about?" he asked.

"They taught us to be honest, helpful to others, and good citizens of our Fatherland. We were also given practical lessons and drills on how to cook a meal, how to sew, et cetera. On our campouts we learned how to survive in the wild."

Kuznetzov listened to me quietly for a while, then broke in, "How often did you meet? Did you believe in all those capitalistic ideals?"

"We usually met once a month," I answered. "The meetings were always exciting and useful. The boy scouts were an important part of my life—"

Kuznetzov cut me off. "What about the Sokol group? What did you do there?"

"We practiced gymnastics and marching. On Polish national holidays, the Third of May Constitution Day, for instance, we took part in the city parade . . ."

I was getting all wound up and was ready to tell him

more, because I had really enjoyed being with my friends there and felt proud of my membership in the Sokol, but the interrogator cut me off and asked me suddenly, "Why did you belong to these organizations?"

"Well, to make friends and to learn practical skills for keeping fit. I liked the active, interesting times we had at the meetings." At this point, he softened his tone of voice and began to talk more like a friend.

Now Kuznetsov seemed genuinely interested in my personal background, my talents, and my ambitions. He wanted to know everything about my friends or playmates—what kind of games or activities we were fond of and what sports we played. He asked me what kind of school I went to, what kind of family I lived with, what plans or dreams for the future I had, and the like. He was amiable and didn't press me for any particular answers. Our conversation was conducted in Russian, since his knowledge of Polish was minimal and I spoke Russian with ease. He wrote copious notes on everything I said, diligently writing down all the names and addresses that I innocently mentioned. He was collecting personal data upon which he could later formulate a psychological attack against me. Based upon what I told him during the investigation, he would determine the most effective charges to be pressed against me.

The first session lasted just over two hours. At the end of the session I still had no idea why I was arrested. I felt secure in thinking that they had no proof of my possession of any contraband weapons, or of my being involved in any illegal or forbidden activities. On the way back to the cell, I still had some hope that I would soon be released and allowed to go home; however, that was childish, naive, wishful thinking.

The second interrogative session came a week later.

This one lasted about five hours. Lieutenant Kuznetzov was again the interrogating officer. He was much more determined to start me talking about more serious things. He told me at the beginning of the session, "I know all about your friends and about all your activities. If you tell me the whole truth about your crimes and confess to everything, I will allow you to go home today and you will be free."

Something kept telling me not to say anything about my own activities or anyone else's. The investigator was not satisfied with my noncooperation. I said to him again, "I've told you all I know. I don't know what other people were doing."

He shouted at me angrily and said that he would have one of my friends at the next hearing to prove that I was a "rotten liar." At other times, in a kinder tone, he promised to help me become a hero of the Soviet Air Force, as I had mentioned to him earlier that I dreamed of becoming a pilot.

Shortly thereafter I had a confrontation with a boy whom I barely remembered meeting at any of our secret gatherings. Edmund Modzelewski looked well groomed, freshly bathed, rested, and healthy. He even wore an attractive necktie and long, neatly combed hair. By contrast, I was emaciated and pale. My hair was cut skin-close, with ridges where the prison barber had missed.

I had lost count of the number of times I had been called out to these interrogations. Some of these sessions lasted four or five hours, at other times my "friendly" Lieutenant Kuznetzov raged and raved at my unwillingness to cooperate with him—then he would hit me in anger, walk out and call in one or two of his assistants who would continue with me in the same angry mood for hours, demanding the names and addresses of various friends, and threatening to kill me if I didn't tell them. Kuznetzov returned, visibly refreshed, his mood changed to friendly again, asking me the same questions, demanding the same truth. The sessions usually ended only when I was totally exhausted and couldn't sit up on the stool any longer. Several sessions went on around the clock, for twenty-five to thirty hours nonstop. By the time Edmund was brought in for confrontation, I had had many sleepless nights, being kept all day and night at interrogations. One such session lasted almost two days and two nights nonstop.

Edmund either didn't know anything about the doings of the NKVD, or else he pretended he didn't know about the devilishly cunning psychological and physical punishments being meted out to the prisoners. Among the methods practiced for extracting confessions was putting a board on the victim's back and hitting the board with a heavy object, such as a piece of pipe or a mallet. This process left no marks on the skin, but caused excruciating pain, separating the flesh from their bones. I observed the effects of this treatment on several prisoners who, upon returning from their interrogative sessions, could not sleep in any position for days. They were in constant pain because of bruised bones and damaged connective tissues. These men tossed back and forth, moaning quietly, trying to find a less painful position. They were warned to not talk about it to anyone, or else they would get even harsher treatment. They were afraid to talk, for there were several stool pigeons in each cell who reported constantly, for promises of more lenient treatment or freedom.

Another favorite method practiced by most investigators was to put the accused into a small dungeon measuring eight feet by six feet. It was sometimes lit by a dim bulb, but there was no bed, and human feces and urine covered the damp cement floor. The terrible stench and the sight of bugs crawling around would usually make the miserable prisoner vomit. No food or drink was given for two or three days, and often the victim would break down and confess, even to things he had never thought of doing, or he would start mentioning other people's names, which pleased the NKVD investigators, who could bring in more people for investigation. It was a constant process, like a chain reaction. Nearly every interrogation resulted in the hunt and arrest of new people. This process was the *modus operandi* of the Soviet secret police, and the key to success was to maintain an unchallengeable control over their victims' minds.

Edmund apparently didn't know about such things yet. He had just come from his home, not from a prison cell. He told the investigators that I frequented patriotic meetings where plans were made to organize underground activities against the victorious Soviet armies and others who came to "protect" the Polish people against the Nazis. I flatly denied all of Edmund's statements and denunciations. I said that I had never seen him before and that I had never attended such meetings.

During that unforgettable hearing in May 1940, which lasted over forty hours, several teams of two or three investigators rotated every four or five hours. Each team began by knocking me around with their hands to wear me out physically and spiritually and to scare me into telling them "the truth." To start with, they had me sit in a chair in the middle of a large room. Several strong floodlights were suspended around me, about four to five feet above my head. Beside my chair was another chair, empty. I wondered at first who was going to sit there, but soon it became apparent that my cunning masters had arranged a confrontation for me. There were six additional investigators brought in for that occasion, and they positioned themselves around me. Lieutenant Kuznetzov was the main interrogator. They wanted me to admit that I had accepted a few pages of the printing font from another member of our group, Thad Lubek. He was a Polish policeman's son. We both worked at the Soviet government printing shop. As the investigators shot various incriminating questions at me, the team posted around me watched every twitch of my muscles, every beat of my pulse, every blink of my eyes, monitoring my reactions to every question. I was nervous from the intense heat and glare of the floodlights converging on me from all sides.

Finally they brought him in. Thad declared, glaring at me with his big bulging eyes, that he had handed to me, on a December evening on the Kosciuszko Bridge, a large, heavy package containing three pages of printing font. I continued to deny, but I was getting near total collapse under the unbearable barrage of pressure.

Kuznetzov boomed further questions at me, "Now tell us, Risha'rd, what did you do with it? To whom did you give it? Tell us, then you'll be a free man. Tell us!"

Thad was still glaring at me, because I had apparently screwed up his plans, as he had expected to be freed as soon as he confronted me publicly and stated the "facts." In addition to the many pressures on me, it was Thad's ridiculously twisted Russian accent, of all things, that made me especially angry at him. He was trying so very hard to be eloquent and lucid, to explain where and when the transfer took place. In his eagerness to please the investigators with facts, Thad was manufacturing his own stories of people whom I had never known and events that had never occurred. When I realized that Thad was either confused or making up a pack of lies, to the point where only a small portion of what he said was true, I denied everything he had ascribed to me or accused me of. Then they sent Thad away, but they kept me for many hours longer, throwing questions at me from all directions. At a certain point, when I was close to the breaking point, I started looking about me with wild eyes and I said to Lieutenant Kuznetzov, "I don't know anything now, citizen investigator. I have forgotten it all."

I must have been hit by one of the men standing around me, because suddenly I felt as if everything were whirling around, and I just collapsed on the floor.

Next they tried a unique experiment on me, calculated to break down my will to resist. After they revived me and put me back on the chair, they brought in a four-legged stool, turned it upside down, sat me on one of the bare legs, and forced me to stretch both of my legs out in front of me. It was more than I could bear. Images flashed through my mind of men impaled on the stake during the Tartar and Turkish invasions of Poland in the Middle Ages. I soon passed out and slid off the stool leg, landing on the floor. I vaguely remember being brought to with a pitcher of cold water. I was roughly picked up by one of the NKVD men and put back on the chair to answer more questions.

The next day, the "harbinger of doom" again came to my cell and shouted, "Letter L."

This time, however, the guard told me to bring all my *veshchi* (possessions). I didn't have any possessions, but it was his routine to say that. I wasn't taken to the investigator's headquarters, but to my next prison home, a solitary dungeon cell in the underground level of the prison. I took my little sack with me, in which I had squirreled away remnants of bread that I had missed eating when I was summoned for interrogation during mealtime. Preceded and followed by guards with automatic weapons, as usual, I was led down several flights of narrow stone stairs. On a straight stretch of corridor the leading guard suddenly stopped and ordered me to stop and face the wall, as other prisoners were being led through the same corridor. We soon reached our destination. The guard unlocked the iron door and shoved me into a dark room.

At first I saw nothing, but I felt cold, damp air on my face. After a few moments my eyes adjusted to the dark, and I saw the "far" wall directly in front of my face. I smelled the stench of human excrement and saw only a dim light coming through a crevice between the water pipes.

Moving sideways, I stepped into a pile of human feces. I slumped down against one wall that felt less wet than the others and fell asleep from exhaustion. There was no way for me to measure the time; I could have slept for a few minutes or for several hours.

I was aroused by a key squeaking in the metal lock, and a guard came in with an aluminum mug of ersatz coffee, lukewarm and unsweetened, and a slice of bread that tasted like sawdust. Without a word, he left this dinner for me and locked the door again. He returned shortly, only to take the aluminum cup from me.

I dozed off again, feeling exhausted and sore after my last interrogative sessions. I wasn't aware of the time—I didn't know whether it was day or night. Besides being tired and sore I also felt drugged by the sour stench of excrement covering the cement floor.

In my half-sleep I heard a key being turned in the keyhole. I jolted back to consciousness. Then I heard a slight commotion by the door and a man was pushed into my room, back first. He argued with the guards, shouting at them in Russian, "Fuck off, you bloody murderers!" But they overpowered him and shoved him inside, his back first, locking the door fast behind him.

Now that he was inside, he turned halfway and tried to focus his eyes through the semidarkness in the dungeon. When he saw me squatting on the floor he spoke, in Polish. "Those rotten sons of bitches, what do they want of me? Why have they brought me into this stinking dump? I haven't done anything, haven't hurt anybody. They keep tormenting me about the names of some of my friends. I don't know anybody here. Why are you here?"

"I don't know," I said.

Then he looked at me more carefully. When I got up from my squatting position, the top of my head reached only to his shoulders. He was still cursing like a trooper, but now his swear words were even more choice, as he mixed Russian, Ukrainian, and Polish profanities, all against the commissar and the guards who put him in this dungeon. After about an hour his raving slowed down and he became interested in me and my background. He introduced himself. "My name is Mieczyslaw, Mietek for short. Where are you from?"

"Lutsk."

"What's your name?"

"Richard."

"So you don't know why they put you in this smelly hole?"

"No, they haven't told me yet. Why are you in here?"

"Well, they locked me up because I was a soldier—fought against the Germans. Oh, I don't know why; maybe it's because our country has lost the war. I was just a soldier in the cavalry squadron near Lodz. We were on horses charging against the German tanks, and we got smashed real bad, then we had to run as fast as we could all the way to Lublin. We had to leave our horses in the woods. The Germans were pelting us with bombs and machine guns from their planes. They kept pressing us further east, until we passed the River Bug. Then our C.O. ordered us to scatter; everyone had to seek his own way for cover. Most of us kept heading east. We heard rumors that the Soviets were our friends, that they would give us shelter and food. When we got to the Volhynia province our men were attacked by Ukrainian bands, no one was safe, singly or in groups. We heard that there were Polish partisan units hiding in the forests, but I didn't have enough time to find any of them."

Mietek said all of that story almost in one breath, because he was still very angry and irritated. He said it all in extreme anger and bitterness, as if he felt the need to get it off his chest. I listened to his harangue as carefully as my tiredness and exhaustion allowed me. After resting a few minutes, Mietek continued telling his story.

"For safety, I chucked my uniform under a bush and got me a civilian outfit I found on the body of a man I stumbled on in the fields. His throat was slashed and the body was already cold, so he didn't need his clothes.

"I joined a loosely organized group of Polish patriots, some former soldiers who were no bloody military men. Some had recently been soldiers and others used to be local government functionaries who had taken to the woods when the NKVD men were sweeping the town of all the 'dangerous' people. These men planned to sabotage the Soviet occupational activities. I thought we could do something against these Asiatic barbarians, but no such luck. My new friends were a wild bunch, without any military leadership. We had no chance to do any good. Then I got separated from them. On one of my reconnaissance patrols I was surrounded by a band of those sneaky Ukrainian villagers plundering and combing through the countryside. They turned me over to the Kalmyks near Kiwerce. Now these no-good bastards want me to tell them the names of the rest of the men from that group. I don't know their bloody names and I don't know where they are. I just don't know nothing."

He kept on talking, to himself mostly, without looking at me or anywhere in particular. He was angry and had to unload his anger. I listened because he talked, but I was still too groggy with fatigue after my recent interrogative sessions to pay much attention to what he said. Then he turned to me and asked, "Hey, Richard, you're just a boy. What could you have done to be put in here?"

I didn't feel like talking to him. I was anxious to rest, as I knew that I could be called out again any time for more questioning. Besides, something closed up in me, and I didn't feel like sharing my affairs with anyone, not even with someone who might be a friend—or perhaps not. He might have been a "plant"—how could I be sure?

So I just said halfheartedly, "I didn't do anything wrong. I belonged to the boy scouts and to the Sokol. The investigator wants to know the names of all my friends, but I don't know their names. I don't know where they are."

"Who was your scoutmaster? Where is he now?"

"I don't know who the scoutmaster was, and I don't know where he is now," I said, feeling more and more uneasy with this guy.

"What about your family? Where are they?"

"I think they are all at home."

I decided not to talk to Mietek any more. "I feel very tired," I told him. "I want to rest."

Mietek was very tired too, and he didn't press any more questions on me. Fatigue overcame us and we both fell hard asleep.

When I awoke, Mietek was no longer with me. I really must have been exhausted to have slept so soundly! In my previous cells I learned to sleep very cautiously, like a cat. I heard almost all that was going on around me—the doors being opened, and men being taken out at all times of the day or night. Even when the guard looked through the judas hole in the door I was aware of it, all the while supposedly sleeping.

The next three or four days I just existed, barely aware of day or night. Twice a day the guard brought a foul-tasting liquid that he called *chiay* (tea) and a slice of very hard, stale bread. I had no choice but to eat it. In the regular cells we had gotten an additional noon meal of watery barley soup, which was ladled out day after day.

My semi-existence ended just as unexpectedly as it started. It was midday when the guard turned his key in the thick door of my little dungeon. All he said was, *Vihodi!* [Come out]"

As soon as I was out of the door, he quickly said, "Face the wall."

There was a convoy of three prisoners being led through the corridor, and again we were subjected to the same procedure of stopping, turning around, and facing the wall—to preserve the secrecy of the whole slave system. We had no choice but follow the orders.

We found out later that, in all parts of the USSR, there seemed to be an insatiable need for slave workers, for the exploitation of mineral and forestry resources.

5
The Ultimate Test

The guard led me through the maze of hallways and crooked stairways to the third floor of the prison building. In a long, narrow room, behind a small desk, sat the familiar Lt. Kuznetzov. Right away, I noticed irritation on his face, as though he was unhappy with the progress of my interrogation. He expressed concern over the deathly pallor in my face. He brought me to a large mirror and said, "Look at yourself. You don't have much life left in you."

Indeed, I was shocked by my own appearance. My eyes seemed to have sunken deep into their sockets, and my cheekbones protruded from an emaciated, withered face. I was sixteen years old, but my face was that of an old man.

However, there was no time for personal reflection. The commissar hadn't summoned me to commiserate over my poor health. He quickly changed his mood and became his normal irritable and insensitive self again. He started telling me again that, if I weren't so stupid and stubborn, he would use all his powers to enable me to become a hero of the Soviet Union, as a pilot or in whatever other profession I would choose.

"Otherwise, if you don't start telling me the names of all your friends and the whole truth about them, I have orders to destroy you, just as so many thousands of unworthy foes of the People's Republic have been destroyed."

After giving me a few minutes for making up my mind, he said, "We have given you plenty of time and chances to come to your good senses and to stop acting stupid. I don't have any more patience for you. You have taken too much of our time. You don't deserve any more."

He was furious. He paced around by his desk for a few moments, then he raised his hand, and pointing to the far end of the narrow office, he shouted at me, "Now, go over there and stand by that wall!"

I noticed that the wall had no pictures or decorations on it, but had a few holes in it.

He was still reminding me that I could yet repent and tell him the "whole truth."

At that time I thought, for the first time in my life, that the feeble, flickering flame of my existence would be extinguished before it had a chance to grow strong again. Suddenly my mind was transformed. I was no longer a youth with vigorous blood and carefree hope flowing through my veins, but a fully mature adult, judging the values of life and death. I was not scared or disappointed. I had done what my aunt Frances taught me, without using so many words. I had done, even then, what I felt was morally right, and I feared no man, nor anything that could harm only my body. It was a peculiar, momentarily frightening feeling which was soon replaced by a sense of complete resignation. No, I was not afraid of what I knew was coming. Indeed, I reasoned with myself, I no longer wished to live in the world which was thrust upon us. If this was to be the new order of things, I would be better off dead. As the commissar uncocked his pistol behind my back he cursed me, and said, "The Soviet society doesn't need fools like you."

Then some wild thoughts rushed through my mind, creating strange pictures that I have never been able to erase from my memory.

I enter a huge hall . . . like an arena. The hall is lighted by powerful floodlights—or is it the rays of the rising sun coming through the clouds? There are seats on all sides of the hall. They are all empty, but I am not alone. I notice two silhouettes standing side by side. I recognize the silhouettes as my mother and her sister, Aunt Frances. They must have come to watch me, to see if I can pass the trial. This is a solemn occasion, like the Final Judgment. I hear a powerful but distant voice, in Russian, asking me to tell the truth. It keeps repeating the same order many times, like an echo bouncing off the sides of the hall.

"Tell the truth or you'll be destroyed."

I still don't know what truth the commissar wants me to tell him, but I think he wants me to give him more information about my family and friends.

My inner voice tells me, however, not to tell him anything else, because I would endanger other people's lives.

I stand in front of him for a while, saying nothing. Then he says, "Go and stand by that wall."

I go toward the wall, stop, and turn around, fearfully expecting further orders.

Then I hear him loudly say,

"Obiernis'licom k'stienie [turn around and face the wall]."

Once more he wants me to tell him more details about my friends—their names, addresses, and what I am doing with them.

"This is your last chance to tell the whole truth or you will perish. We don't need fools like you. We will destroy you!"

I hear beautiful singing up above. Who is that singing?

The silhouettes still watch me. They shake their heads as if to tell me not to say any more. I have already decided not to talk. My life isn't worth saving if it's to be the kind of life that our enemies have forced upon us.

A strange sensation comes over me. I feel as if my life were running at an accelerated pace—I see pictures moving on a large panoramic screen in front of me.

At the beginning I see myself as a small child three or four years old, in Warsaw, playing under a bridge on the River Vistula, where fishermen catch fish and crabs. My sick mother comes across and looks sadly at me. I want to reach out and touch her, grab her hand, but the picture moves on constantly. A few moments later I see myself sitting on a train, on the way to Lutsk, looking out at the wide open fields of rye waving gently in the June breeze.

The pictures move on. Now I am in school. Mr. Red'ko smiles at me benignly, his goatee shaking slightly. Now I am an altar boy in the Lutsk Cathedral. Now the beach by the River Styr appears and I show off my bicycle trick-riding. I feel that my life is quickly coming to an end, but I am neither sorry nor afraid of the change. I have had a happy life. I have fulfilled my mission, though I'm not sure what it was. Now it's not up to me to choose whether I am to live or die. Instinctively I say, "Oh, God of my Fathers. You decide what is to happen to me. Thy will be done."

I hear a sharp, clapping sound. Something hit the wall, close to my head. I see another hole in the wall. Then there is the same sound again—another hole in the wall. The clapping keeps echoing in my ears, louder and louder. I feel woozy and faint. I try to look around and touch my arms, to make sure I am still here—or is this the other place? The silhouettes are still watching me. They show signs of approval. What have I done? I hear singing again. Where am I? I'm tired and confused. The silhouettes fade. The singing stops.

I hear the commissar-interrogator's voice very close to me. I faintly make out his words.

"I've decided to spare your life. But you are a fool. You've nothing to fight for, and we'll reeducate you. You will still become a hero of the Soviet Air Force, and a proud citizen of our Fatherland."

I hear my own voice now. "Maybe, commissar-interrogator, maybe. But I am tired now. Please, let me sit down."

He leads me back to his desk. Slowly, I sit on a chair. He claps his hands and the guard comes in. The commissar orders him to take me away.

We did not, however, return to my dungeon cell. Evidently the investigator had decided that I would not last much longer in the dungeon. The guard put me in a small room on the second floor, which had a little window near the ceiling. Real daylight came through. There was even a wooden floor and a cot in the room, luxuries I could only dream about in my previous cell. It didn't take much to make one happy under the circumstances in that prison.

The same day, about three hours later, an unexpectedly pleasant surprise came to me. The cell door opened and a sack was delivered, full of exquisite delicacies. The guard said,

"Eto dla tiebia [this is for you]." I opened the sack and began to pull out various food items.

There were two loaves of bread, some cheese, sausage, butter, and even some fruit. There were also cigarettes, but I no longer had any interest in smoking.

I could not believe my eyes! Who sent this generous parcel? Who could afford to buy them, at the black market prices? Who could find them? There were not many things available in the stores before I was arrested.

I found out much later that my sister had tried many times to deliver a parcel to me, but the investigator repeatedly refused to allow any parcel to be delivered to me, as a means of punishing me for noncooperation. I don't believe that the commissar was moved in any way by my haggard and sickly appearance. He may have been afraid that I might not survive much longer, and the Soviets might lose a future "hero." My investigator, Lieutenant Kuznetsov, was still telling me that they (the Soviet authorities) would reeducate me and train me to become an ace pilot, if I confessed the "whole truth." For that reason he may have allowed the food parcel to be brought to me. I began to feel soreness in my chest, I had difficulty breathing, and I no longer craved nicotine. Later on, I exchanged the cigarettes with another prisoner for some food.

Three days later I was transferred again, this time to an entirely different type of cell. As I was led into a room on the second floor of the west side of the prison complex, the first thing I noticed was a comparatively large, barred window, bricked up to about six feet from the floor.

I had a peculiar notion that, since this was a brand new room for me, if I had a dream during my first night in this room, it would be a very significant one. Being in this room almost made me feel happy. I looked forward to my first night's sleep in it.

It was strange, I thought later, that it is not how many of the worldly goods a person has that makes him happy with his lot, but, rather, it is the amount of improvement from what the person has had right along, as well as our expectations of improvement in the future—that is what brings people out of depression. My recent good fortune—the food parcel—had almost entirely cancelled out the brutal abuse I had suffered. I was almost happy.

Now, I had eaten some good food, was allowed to rest almost as much as I needed, and my resignation and depression were gone.

My first day in cell 203 was filled with new experiences. I made several new acquaintances and learned about the fate of some of my friends in other cells. Most of the inmates in this new cell were political prisoners, i.e., people whom the NKVD had classified as the "enemies of the people," such as policemen, government clerks and other officials, teachers, former soldiers, and the like. In the afternoon, out of curiosity I raised myself up to the window bars to look outside. The view was beautiful. The River Styr flowed very near the prison complex, on its eastern side. Beyond the river lay a verdant meadow, a few miles wide, dotted with patches of white and yellow primroses, dandelions, and blue forget-me-nots.

There was not much more floor space per prisoner in this cell than in the other cells, but somehow this room seemed more spacious. The prisoners seemed more relaxed and less harassed. In the daytime some of the mattresses were piled up along the walls so as to clear an area in the middle of the room where the inmates could walk around. Sitting motionless for days, weeks, or months caused stiffness and soreness in the joints and muscles. The walks were conducted single-file, in a circular pattern, to avoid excessive congestion. Now it was about the middle of summer, 1940; some prisoners had been in that prison for as long as ten or eleven months. Apart from a short walk in the prison yard or a trip to the state police offices for investigation, those men had not left the prison walls.

In this cell, most of the inmates slept on bare mattresses on the floor. The less fortunate ones used whatever articles of outer clothing they had—an overcoat, a jacket, or an old fur—to serve simultaneously as a mattress, a pillow, and a blanket. Those inhabitants of the cell who had been in it for the longest time inherited their mattresses from inmates who were removed from the cell for various dispositions. I was lucky. Two men, each of whom had a mattress in the middle section of the room, must have felt compassion for me.

They pushed their mattresses close together and let me sleep on the joint between them. It was much more comfortable than sleeping on the hard wooden floor, which would have been my lot as a newcomer. Since the inmates had to lie close to each other, they decided that it was healthier to sleep with every other man's head near the feet of his two neighbors. The smell of unwashed feet was thought to be less harmful than exhaled carbon dioxide! I have, since then, found out that this practice had sound basis in fact, even though no one in the prison cell at that time could explain this phenomenon scientifically.

I slept soundly that night and, as expected, had a beautiful, hope-inspiring dream. I dreamed that the iron bars on the window were ripped away by some superhuman, invisible power, leaving a huge hole in the prison wall. However, none of the inmates tried to escape, because across the river there was a splendid show being performed. It was a beautiful, sunny day. On the flowered meadow there was a man on a white horse. He rode around the meadow in wide circles and sang, in a joyous, powerful tenor, the romantic aria from Moniuszko's opera *Lalka*. I was enchanted by the magnificence of this spectacle on the spacious, natural stage. The meadow was richly embroidered with multicolored flowers, with a huge rainbow at one end of the horizon, and bright noon sunlight illuminating the entire scene.

When I awoke the next morning my reality had not changed, but my spirits were lifted by my dream of the previous night. "Bukfa L [Letter *L*],' my last name initial, was called after I had barely finished the morning meal of barley and a mug of ersatz coffee. I was taken to the NKVD headquarters for more questioning. The procedure was the same; the investigator kept demanding more information, there were more physical and psychological tortures and more promises. The NKVD man wanted me to confess that I had stolen some printing font, but since none was found at my home, I decided not to divulge any more information, regardless of the pressure exerted on me. This session was relatively short, it lasted only about four hours. Then the guards brought me back to the cell.

There was a man in cell 203 whom I befriended accidentally, and in whom I confided about my investigative sessions. He was in his mid-thirties, a ship captain in the Polish Navy, who was arrested by NKVD agents while visiting his father in Lutsk. His father was well known to me, as he was our family physician, Dr. Gudzinov. Dr. Gudzinov was highly respected and trusted by the entire town, and I instinctively began to trust his son. For me, a boy barely sixteen years of age, the pressures of physical and psychological tortures applied by the NKVD sleuths were exhausting my body and my nerves. I had to seek out friendly souls among the adult political prisoners.

One day I was indicted by the allegations of an NKVD witness, a former playmate and "colleague in crime." He told the investigators that he had given me some printing font and ammunition, describing the exact circumstances under which the transaction had supposedly taken place. After over thirty straight hours of nonstop brutal questioning and several hours of confrontation with the witness, Thad Lubek, I collapsed in the investigator's office. I knew that I couldn't tell the truth, because that would immediately involve my whole family and many other people. I was in a quandary. When I came to, I was taken back to the cell. I decided to talk to Captain Gudzinov—maybe he could suggest a way out for me.

We walked around the cell, that being the safest way

to communicate without being overheard by the NKVD spies planted in the cell. As I explained my plight to the captain, he came up with a solution. He suggested that I pretend that I had lost my sanity. Suddenly he whispered to me, "We are being watched by a spy. Say, 'Ah,' as I look down your throat." I did as I was told, as he was much more experienced in these matters than I. He pretended to give me some advice on my "sore throat." Then we continued walking around the cell.

That afternoon I was called out for a hearing in the prison office and was grilled by the investigator about the very thing Captain Gudzinov and I had talked about in the cell! The investigator told me that Captain Gudzinov had informed the interrogator that I told him that I had accepted the font. I was dumbfounded, puzzled. Would he really betray me? But I had trusted Captain Gudzinov, and, against great odds, I decided to assume that it was another ploy that the NKVD man was using on me. My hope and trust in the captain's character, even though he had been called out of the cell earlier that afternoon, was complete and unshaken. In this weird predicament, I remembered his advice to me. I started mumbling incoherently and stared around wildly. Somehow, as if involuntarily, I started saying to the officer, "Nichevo ne znayu, pozvoltie otdohnut [I don't know anything; let me rest]." Then I slid off the chair and collapsed. When I came to, the officer had me returned to the cell.

Then came a break in my interrogations. Apparently the NKVD men concluded that they could not get any more confessions out of me. I was completely exhausted, physically broken, and had convinced them that I was no longer mentally coherent. The investigation of our group's case was nearing a conclusion. The investigators had collected enough information on us and on all our families.

They would round up new groups of people, arrest and interrogate them, and get a few hundred more victims for the Siberian slave labor camps. Any demonstration of loyalty to Poland was considered counterrevolutionary and anti-Soviet, and punishable to the highest degree.

Prison Life

6

Since my interrogations appeared to have stopped for the moment, I had more time to participate in the social life of the cell community, which was by no means boring. There were always the frequent interruptions by the "harbinger of doom." Sometimes when he called out the initial of a person's last name, several people responded with their names before he heard the name he wanted.

Six months passed, from March to September, during which time I was mostly concerned with my own survival, because of frequent beatings during the interrogations, being deprived of regular sleep or meals for two or three days at a time, and the psychological tortures by teams of interrogators. They finally must have decided that they couldn't extract any more confessions out of me. They closed our group's case and made it ready for the court to decide our fate. I had a chance to catch up on my sleep and to look around the cell to see how my cellmates were passing their time.

Among the pastimes were checkers and chess games, in which several men were real champions. Every so often the leaders in the cell organized chess or checkers tournaments. There were no tangible prizes to be won, but the participants in the games were very serious about their game. The checkers and chess figurines were made out of bread by resident artists. The bread was slightly moistened and pressed by hand until it became completely moldable.

Then an artist shaped the figurines to resemble the finest quality store-bought chess figures. For the black set, paper or rags were burned to provide soot for the black coloring. The chess board was drawn and painted with soot in a less conspicuous place on the floor, so that the guard would not be likely to notice it. Every time there was a hot game between two skilled contestants, there were several anxious voices rooting for their favorite.

Another game we played was one called "I Have a Secret." In this game one of the participants would pick an object, an event, or an idea and keep it as his secret, to be shared with one other person, who would serve as a referee. The rest would take turns at guessing what the secret was by progressively eliminating categories of objects or ideas until someone could zero in and identify the secret by its correct name. This game attracted all the inmates in the cell to participate. It was intellectually stimulating as well as very entertaining.

The most popular pastime by far, however, was lectures given by inmates, experts in various fields of academic or professional specialization. Among the political prisoners were many who could recite whole novels in a serial fashion, over a period of several days. These men of letters recited either their own novels or mysteries, which they created as they went along, works written by our favorite national authors and poets, or works by international masters in Polish translations. Historians gave lectures on ancient, medieval, or contemporary history. Lectures on ancient Greek history that were given in cell 203 have stayed fresh in my memory for over forty years, since they were given in such a fascinating manner. They

aroused in me a long-standing love for history.
These lectures were conducted from the beginning of my stay in cell 203. At first, whenever the guards saw us through the "judas" in the door, sitting quietly, listening attentively to one person from amongst our group, they broke up our lectures. We quickly devised an alternate plan. The same lectures were conducted while the lecturer and the listeners walked around the middle of the floor. The same procedure was used for group prayers, which were conducted by a fellow-prisoner priest in our midst.

While the NKVD authorities tried very persistently, and most often successfully, to isolate the prisoners from one another so as to make their communication as difficult as possible, the prisoners developed an internal system of communicating across the prison walls. This system utilized a modified Morse code, like the type used by the telegraph service. The prison Morse code, a twenty-five-letter alphabet, was sent through the prison walls, which in some sections of this medieval fortresslike structure were as thick as ten feet. To make the sound travel through the brick wall a metal spoon was used to tap the code. The words were tapped letter by letter, and the person on the receiving end assembled the words by either writing on a slate or, more often, by mentally forming the words and sentences. To improve reception, a metal dinner plate was placed on the wall, with the rim of the plate against the wall. The listener would then put his ear to the plate, which acted as a hearing aid, collecting the sounds traveling across the brick wall and magnifying them. The resulting signal could be received with almost unbelievable clarity.

Here is how the prison Morse code was organized:

		COLUMNS				
		1	2	3	4	5
	1	A	B	C	D	E
	2	F	G	H	I	J
ROWS	3	K	L	M	N	O
	4	P	R	S	T	U
	5	V	W	X	Y	Z

The first group of taps indicated the row number of the letter. After a pause, a second group of taps indicated the column number. For example, the word *able* was transmitted as follows:

. (pause) .
. (pause) . .
. . . (pause) . .
. (pause) . . . . .

It was a tedious and time-consuming method of communication, but we certainly had plenty of time, and messages got through every day.

Time passed slowly, inexorably, only occasionally varied by the messenger guard who came into the cell at odd times of the day or night to call prisoners out. Men returning from interrogations bore signs of brutal treatment. On rare occasions a man might have bruises on his face or a black eye, but usually the board method was used, leaving no visible marks on the outer skin. In this method, a board was placed on the prisoner's body, back or front, and the special interrogator hit the board with a heavy stick or hammer, causing the flesh to almost separate from the bone. These men didn't talk to anyone upon their return. They would just lie quietly for hours, in a dull stupor, only faintly aware of their surroundings.

Other men were subjected to various psychological tortures. In one method, the prisoner was kept in the investigator's quarters for twenty to thirty hours without food or water and then subjected to exhausting questioning. Sometimes the man being questioned would hear the voices of his loved ones and smell the aroma of his favorite dishes from an adjacent room where the door had been left open deliberately. The prisoner was hungry and thirsty and, of course, yearned to see and talk to his relatives, but he was told, "First answer our questions. Tell us what we want to know about your friends and your activities, then you will be allowed to see and talk with your visitors and have a good meal." Obviously, more often than not, the prisoner ended up not being allowed to see his visitors. Often this was after having been away from home for many months, and sometimes the relatives were brought many miles, from a distant town. In many cases, the person being interrogated, from mere exhaustion, and driven like a wild animal by the scent of his favorite dish, would break down and give out names, so as to be allowed to go back to his cell. Some prisoners were smart enough to give phony names or wrong addresses.

One time a boy younger than I was shoved into our cell. He had a large, round head with light reddish hair, about three-quarters of an inch in length, having grown out since being cut by the prison barber. His freckled face was well known to me, as he was a close friend of mine, but it was without the broad smile he always used to wear. We knew each other very well, having been in the same clandestine group. He looked so young and still appeared to have baby fat on his face and body. He was popularly known as Freckled Face. His name was Stas Skowronek.

In my interrogation sessions I stated that the name of Skowronek meant nothing to me. I assumed that little Stas had said the same about me to his investigator. Instinctively, we acknowledged each other only with our eyes at first. We did not speak to each other until the next day. Then we gradually saw each other diffidently, and exchanged a few general introductory remarks, showing only casual interest, as if only because we were the two youngest inmates in that cell. We had to appear casual in approaching each other so that the NKVD spies in the cell would not guess that we had known each other before; thus, we circumvented the attention of those who were watching us and reporting our mutual behavior to the investigators. This circumstance allowed us to enjoy each other's company for several weeks and to share many useful confidences concerning the progress of our cases. Sometimes we were able to warn each other about certain upcoming hearings, which helped us in planning what to say or what not to say, or what to admit and what to deny.

The last month of our group's investigation was spent in a routine existence. Ersatz coffee in the morning, tasteless barley soup twice a day, and some time spent in flea and lice hunting. The weeks passed uneventfully.

On one of the last days of October 1940, Stas Skowronek and I were surprised by being taken out together. The guard took us to the prison office.

"Did they find anything in your house?" Stas asked me.

"No," I replied.

"Did they take anybody else from your family?"

"No, not as far as I know."

Both of us had admitted to nothing. We pleaded total innocence, and nothing was proven against us. We were quite confident that we would soon be set free and allowed to go home. In fact, we thought that it would happen that day. The guard put us into an unmarked NKVD van. As soon as it started moving, we sensed that we were not headed in the direction of home.

We soon arrived at the People's Courthouse. We disembarked from the van and were led into the courthouse by heavily armed guards carrying submachine guns at the ready. There had been ten members in our group, and we were all assembled. Three were ages sixteen to seventeen, four were ages fourteen to sixteen, and three were ages twelve to thirteen. Stas Skowronek was then thirteen years old. I had just turned sixteen.

On the court chamber wall was a huge sign, in Ukrainian, proclaiming deep gratitude to the victorious Soviet Army for liberating the Ukraine from Polish capitalistic oppression. There were about fifteen rows of seats on a sloping floor, separated by an aisle in the middle. We were led directly to the two front rows on the left side of the room. Two soldiers guarded the entrance inside the courtroom, and several heavily armed guards were placed outside the front entrance.

Some spectators were sitting in the last few rows. This was one of the many show trials open to the public, to show how the new Ukrainian Socialist Republic was dealing with "enemies of the people." I didn't recognize anyone among the spectators.

The People's Court prosecutor opened the trial by denouncing the accused boys as traitors and enemies of the Revolution who were sabotaging the People's Army's noble efforts to win a new life for the oppressed masses of workers. No mention was made about the Soviet Army being murderous invaders in our land. It was a trial conducted by the local Polish puppet "self-government" set up by the invading army. The entire proceedings were being watched carefully by the NKVD agents, backed up by their armed guards. The NKVD had gathered some Polish malcontent rabble rousers, criminals of many shades, allowed them to steal and murder whomever they didn't like, and gave them complete military support in case they encountered too strong an opposition. Thus established, the new "Polish People's Government" was in total control of life and death of fellow citizens.

The prosecutor demanded the most severe punishment for all of us—that meant the death penalty. The indictment cited Articles 54 and 58 of the USSR Criminal Code. Article 54 spoke of armed opposition against the People's Revolution. In most of our cases the indictments were accusations of hoarding weapons and ammunition, and of conspiratorial activities against the Soviet People's Army. Allegedly, the weapons were found buried in the woods or in backyards, or sunk in the small lakes around the country.

Article 58 spoke of unfriendly and damaging propaganda against the cause of the Revolution. In the minds of the originators of the Bolshevik Revolution in Russia in 1917, and in the minds of their philosophical heirs throughout the world, there is a continuous need for class struggle. The traditional, governing wealthy social classes must be destroyed by revolution, and a new social class of leaders has to rise from the bottom of society to assume leadership. The new leaders are not to be chosen according to their abilities, but by the degree of their former deprivation (or that of their parents).

In our mock trial we were all charged with the maximum sentence under both Articles 54 and 58. Our public defense lawyer confirmed our guilt and agreed with the prosecutor that we were all public enemies and enemies of the Revolution, but he pleaded with the People's judge to consider our youth and the probability that we would all learn the real truth in time and submit to new teachings and rehabilitation. The latter, he said, could best be done in the corrective camps of the USSR. Two of the three oldest boys were proven guilty and were to die. The third, Zenon K., admitted nothing and had nothing proven against him, but because he had been involved in the activities of the group and had gone through the investigative process, the judge assumed he was guilty. He was sentenced to ten years of hard labor in the rehabilitational camps in Siberia.

The decree sentencing us used the term, in the Russo-Ukrainian language, *pierevospitatielniye laghiera*, which literally means "re-educational camps." All adults taken prisoners in the Russian-occupied countries, mostly for political offenses, with the exception of those killed in the prisons, ended up in the hard-labor camps. There were many thousands of these camps. They still exist now in the eastern stretches of European Russia and in all parts of Siberia. The labor camps are an integral part of the Soviet political system, because they are a very effective way of getting rid of people who are ideologically unsafe. People sent to the camps for any transgressions against the law, real or trumped up, very seldom get out of them to return back into normal civilian life.

Not much had been proven against the next four boys, but circumstantial evidence was collected from the statements of others accused. Included here was Edmund Modzelewski, one who had denounced the whole group, having been promised freedom if he would testify against the others. Thad Lubek, who denounced me, and I were in this group. Three out of this group received sentences of ten years in labor camps in Siberia.

I received only an eight-year sentence of hard labor in a camp in Siberia because no evidence was found in my aunt's house and nothing was proven against me. My aunt Frances's son Chester ran away to the city of Lvov right after my arrest and thus was spared the arrest and all subsequent meetings with the NKVD agents.

Stas Skowronek was pronounced innocent because nobody had implicated him during the investigations, but he was not allowed to join his family in Lutsk again. For some strange reason, Stas seemed the most unhappy and began to cry in the courtroom. His round, freckled face became very long and sad. Through his sobbing, he explained to the judge that he wanted to go with the rest of us and did not want to be sent to a resettlement camp in the Asian territory of Kazakhstan as the judge had recommended. I have never come across any news of Stas, and don't know where he ended up, or if he has survived. The remaining two boys in the youngest group received sentences of ten years in re-educational camps in the USSR for young offenders.

The severe court sentences of the People's Court didn't register in our minds right away. We just could not believe that two out of our group of ten had been sentenced to death—they were executed that same month. No appeals were allowed from the verdicts of the People's Court. In those terrible, hectic war years there was no time to be wasted on such formalities. The main idea was to kill off all alleged leaders of any budding conspiratorial movement.

Thus the People's judge disposed of our small group of ten counterrevolutionaries who dared to dream of fighting for the freedom of their country. There was still hope for us to be rehabilitated in the vast slave camps of Siberia.

If our minds couldn't be reshaped, we would perish. If there were any obstacles or severe problems blocking this process, we would still be fated for destruction. We were returned to our prison cells to collect our sacks of possessions. After the sentences were pronounced, the judge closed our cases. We were all returned, under much increased security, back to our prison cells. A day or two after our return from the People's Court we found ourselves together in one large "transport" cell, number 300. We thought only the Polish political activists would be there, but there were almost as many Polish Ukrainians. We had all been designated by the NKVD commissars to be shipped to the farthest eastern area of the USSR. The NKVD was exceptionally efficient in processing those sentenced by the People's Court. No delays were allowed, because thousands more had to be processed and disposed of.

The short time that we were to stay in cell 300 was not very peaceful. There were large numbers of Ukrainian nationalist freedom fighters. Prior to 1939, they had fought against the Polish government established in 1918. These Ukrainian freedom fighters had helped the invading Soviet army disarm and kill thousands of Polish soldiers. The Poles were retreating from the overwhelming onslaught of the German panzer divisions and from the German bombers who were machine-gunning defenseless civilians fleeing from the constantly shifting war zones. After the Soviets strengthened and solidifed their position on the Polish soil, they turned their attention to the Ukrainians, the Jews, and the Bielorussians.

Soviets did not like any type of national freedom fighters, because such people had the tendency to nurture ideas of independence for themselves. To the Russians, such daring ideas are intolerable. Soon the Ukrainian patriots, who were strongly anti-Poland, found themselves side by side with Polish freedom fighters in the Soviet prisons. Therefore, there were plenty of old resentments mixed with strong, Soviet-inspired hostilities. Even though we were all mistreated by the Soviet guards, there was still enough energy left in the cellmates to start vicious verbal and physical assaults, one group against the other. Cell 300 became a battlefield between the Ukrainian patriots and the Polish zealots. On three occasions during the final two weeks of our stay in cell 300, various objects, such as heavy boots or metal plates, were tossed by the inmates of one side at those on the other side.

We were visited several times in the last two weeks of November by a prison commissar, Korenninkov, partly to pacify the hot tempers in the cell so that inmates would not start an open fight. Another reason for visits by *Kapusta* (we called him Cabbagehead, since his head was totally bald) to cell 300 was to inform us of our upcoming journey. He told us it would be a long journey and a difficult one. Among other items of information, he told us, in very vulgar Russian terms, "Zhit' buditie, no gulat' nie s'hatitie! [You may survive, but you won't feel like enjoying yourselves!]" Indeed, the whole aim of our oppressors was to squeeze all the joy of our life out of us, all our hopes and dreams. This was to be accomplished gradually, by hard conditions of life, starvation, and constant fear of death, so our thoughts would be consumed just by the efforts to hold on to life. As we found out later by observing Soviet prisoners and living conditions of Soviet "free" people, that this was the essence of the Soviet social philosophy—the instilling of the fear of authority into their subjects and isolating them from the world of freedom. Then they have no choice but to say that they like what they have.

We all felt deep anguish and, at the same time, desperate helplessness. If we had any chance at all, we would have fought back, but under the circumstances, any sign of protest could have been taken for a rebellion. Those guards didn't need much of an excuse or provocation to start shooting and killing innocent people, so we just stood there and said nothing.

7
The Long Journey

Within days of the court's verdict for us on December 1, 1940, the local NKVD authorities set about carrying out the court's orders. They provided the military personnel trucks. They told us to get ready *z vieshchami*, (with our possessions), which always meant that we were leaving the place for good. They took thousands of prisoners to the freight trains, meant for transporting cattle and other livestock and goods, waiting ready at the railway station. Every day the trains were filled with prisoners and started rolling to the vast Soviet eastern European and Asiatic territories, to the thousands of slave-labor camps scattered around the Soviet Union.

Thus started our long journey to the Far East. Our long train, consisting of about 120 cars, was one of many hundreds of such trains, which slowly rode to the east. Each car was filled up to the point of bursting, containing sixty persons, on the average. None of us knew where we were being taken. We were completely at the mercy of the cruel and relentless guards who, in many cases, were shooting at the prisoners just for personal entertainment, or for maintaining the atmosphere of fear and intimidation so that the prisoners wouldn't even think about organizing any resistance. Thousands of slave-labor camps are scattered and operated throughout the vast European and Asian territories of the USSR. They are always in need of a slave-labor force, because most of the slaves cannot survive the unbearable conditions of work for very long, especially on the very meager and insufficient food rations. On the morning of December 1, 1940, we were awakened very early. A guard came to our cell and told us to pack up all our possessions and get ready. My aunt's family and my sister knew that our group had been sentenced and would most likely be transported soon to the Soviet labor camps in the east. Just a week earlier I had received a large sack full of food and extra clothing. Among other things, there was a very old, oversized jacket made out of goatskin, with long, white goat hair on the inside. That turned out to be a memorable fur, because it traveled thousands of miles and protected me from the unbelievably cold arctic winters. It was a gift from Uncle Hieronim, my aunt Frances's husband. He had had it for over twenty years, and was very attached to it. This ancient goat fur had gone with him through the Russian Revolution of 1917. By frequent visits to the local NKVD office, my sister found out about my sentence of eight years of hard labor in the camps in far eastern Siberia. She got that information not from the official authorities, because they never gave out that kind of information, but from people whom she met casually in and around the NKVD offices. My uncle knew that I would need the warm coat. It saved my life many times. Someday in the past, that fur must have been new, but in all my living memory, it had always been old-looking. As a child I had estimated its age at about 150–200 years—certainly at least 100!

While we were packing our things, guesses were circulating about our possible destination. Some inmates had already received advance information that transports of hundreds of thousands of people from Poland were being taken directly to far eastern Siberia. This was just gossip and rumor, not yet official news.

Just then I remembered some paintings I had seen in school, done by a Polish painter by the name of Grottger. They depicted large groups of Polish freedom fighters who had been arrested and sentenced to long-term (twenty-five to thirty years) banishment in the vast stretches of Siberia by the Tsarist soldiers in the January Uprising of 1863. In Polish history classes we learned about the many thousands of Polish men and some women who were taken prisoner in the prime of their life. This was common throughout the 125 years of Russian occupation in Poland. The pictures by Grottger showed hundreds of men in snowy blizzards, in subzero temperatures, stretched out in a single-file line miles long. Some were falling behind the rest of the group from exhaustion, putting forth the last reserves of their strength to survive perhaps another half a mile. They were urged on by guards with whips and knouts. A knout is a special kind of whip, with something heavy attached to the tip to inflict more pain. The guards were mounted on small Siberian horses and were assisted by vicious wolf-dogs. The prisoners were like a herd of cattle being driven to slaughter by cowboys.

Now, in the middle of the twentieth century, our captors used modern techniques—we were to be taken away in trains because they were more efficient. The NKVD agents wrenched hundreds of fathers and sons from their loved ones in the darkness of the night. They transported them directly to the prison in unmarked police vans. The arresting NKVD officers told the frightened families that their men were just being taken for questioning, but the families never saw them again. They used cunning, mean lies, and tricks all the time. Prison cells filled quickly. Floor sleeping space was growing scarce. The terrorized men were collected and large army personnel trucks took them to the long lines of cattle trains (box cars) that were specially prepared and waiting at the railroad siding. At many points along the Russo-European railroad, trains packed with ten to twelve thousand prisoners were pulling away to the east constantly to destinations unknown.

We were ordered out of the cell by several special guards with submachine guns. They closely packed us onto an NKVD truck covered with heavy, dark green tarpaulins. Three guards were seated at the back with submachine guns at the ready. One guard announced before we started off, "If you make any move or any noise, we'll shoot you all without warning."

We all knew they would do it. Several medium-sized trucks were loaded in a hurry, as if time were running out for our captors. The convoy so assembled was set in motion immediately. Two guards sat, one at each outside corner, with a clear view of us inside, as well as a view of the streets along the way. The rear flaps were open, and we were also able to see where we were being taken. The route led directly to the railroad station, via Jagiellonska Street, the city's main thoroughfare. We drove past the cathedral and the former provincial capital headquarters. The latter was still in ruins from German bombs.

I was filled with helpless anger and cried silently. In desperation I thought to myself, *Where is our God now? Doesn't He know that we need His help? Did we trust Him too much?*

Terror froze our thoughts and our emotions. We didn't dare defy the brutal force because that would have meant an instant massacre of us all. Like frightened, disoriented sheep, we succumbed to an uncertain future.

That was the last time I ever viewed the city that had given me so much happiness. The memories of the years past were vividly running through my mind, like the buildings and the trees that we passed standing on each side of the road. Many buildings along the route were totally flattened. Even the skeletons of the structures had been taken apart because people needed bricks and other materials to make repairs on their own damaged homes. The city's brick factory had not reopened after it had been bombed.

The Germans had crippled the city's structures and devastated the architectural inheritance of centuries. Now the Soviet barbarians were depopulating the country of its sons and daughters, as if to make sure that there would be no one to rebuild the cities.

"Why?" we all asked. "For whose sins?"

These depressing thoughts ran through our minds and hearts, and there was hardly any talk among the prisoners. I prayed to my guardian angel not to leave me unprotected and to give me strength to survive the ordeal. We soon reached the Lutsk railway station.

To our great surprise, there was a large group of mourners and well-wishers gathered at the side of the station to bid farewell to their fathers, brothers, and sons. People had found out what time the transports were leaving, in spite of the total secrecy under which all these procedures were carried out. As I stood in line approaching the rear platform, I caught a glimpse of my cousin and my sister Marysia standing in the crowd. They wiped their eyes. Our eyes met fleetingly and we waved to each other. We could not even say good-bye to each other. We were separated by a cordon of guards heavily armed with semi-automatic weapons, who kept the crowds of relatives at a distance from us.

The image of relatives standing near the railway station, with their tearful eyes, quivering mouths, and faces full of subdued anger and helplessness, is still fresh in my mind. They watched their children being taken away for destruction. What was their crime? Their guilt? Why were we not allowed to pause for even a brief, silent good-bye? The guards' rifle butts pushed us on. A train of about 120 cars, barely fit for transporting cattle, even in a fair climate, was soon filled with about sixty bodies per car. Inside each car there were two shelves of wooden planks on each end for sleeping.

In the darkness of that night, December 2, the last car was filled up to capacity and we heard the screeching wheels of the train. The 120-car-long snake shook its vertebrae, as if to check its strength to pull such a load. Then we started to move. First we headed west, circling the city, then we turned east, which was to be our direction for many weeks.

The train cars were constructed for transporting domestic farm animals, such as cattle, pigs, sheep, et cetera, but for the war exigencies, they had been quickly converted for transporting human cargo.

Most of the prisoners were forced to spend much of their waking hours on the shelves, because the stand-up area in the middle of the car could not accommodate more than a third of the occupants. There were two wide sliding doors, one on each side of the car. One door served for the delivery of the daily rations. These rations consisted of one or two slices of dark rye bread and a bowl of soup each. The soup was cooked in a huge thirty-gallon kettle. It was made out of some little salted fish and shredded cabbage, but unfortunately, we rarely saw either the fish or the shreds of cabbage—only their taste was still in the soup. The distribution of these rations depended wholly on whether the station commandant had any spare food supplies and a mind to distribute them to these "enemies of the people."

As we went farther east, away from Lutsk, the supplies of those who had their own food decreased rapidly. One day after leaving Lutsk, we noticed the sign for Zhitomir, the name of a town in the Soviet territory. The train didn't stop at Zhitomir; we continued in a southeasterly direction. We crossed the Dnieper, a wide river, which meant we were going to Kiev.

In about a day we reached Kiev. We stopped, but only as a layover on a siding railroad depot track. Our carriage had no windows, so we could see only fractional pictures of the station grounds through cracks in the walls. By that time we had exhausted most of our food supplies. Our water, held in a twenty-five–thirty-gallon can, was depleted. We had received neither food nor water since we began our journey in Lutsk. The fuel supply for heat in our car had also been exhausted. We shouted alternately to the guards, "Vodi [water!]," "Hleba! [bread!]," or Uhgla! [coal!]," while the train was in motion, knowing full well that no one would hear us. We were desperate. People were in agony; some were fainting.

We renewed our shouting when the train stopped in the side depot, but no guard would open the door. We saw them standing near our car door, but they had their orders and wouldn't budge, even if they wanted to help.

While in the Kiev station, we saw several long trains similar to ours. From hearing the people talking and shouting for essential supplies we knew that they were from various parts of eastern Poland. Our train stood in the station a whole day and part of the night, but the guards found neither time nor compassion to alleviate our misery. Late in the evening, close to midnight, the train began to move back and forth in preparation for being put back on the eastbound tracks. None of us could understand why we had stopped at the Kiev station; perhaps they had added more cars to our train.

The next leg of our journey lasted more than two days. The hunger, thirst, and cold became intolerable. Some fainted or simply fell asleep, exhausted by the unbearable conditions. We were entirely at the mercy of the guards; they could have starved us all to death. With the lack of water and the freezing temperatures in the car, it would not have taken many days to accomplish it.

One morning I was awakened by the extreme cold. I was still wearing my uncle's big goatskin jacket, but I couldn't move away from the wall of the boxcar. I had frozen to the wall, through the fur jacket. I could not believe it. My fellow inmates had to pull me loose, and my entire left side felt numb.

Near Poltava we stopped again. The guards brought a huge kettle on wheels and proceeded to ladle out soup that looked like it contained barley. It tasted like salted fish, but the fish was entirely boiled out. We could see circles of fish grease floating on the surface. The soup was quite salty, which made us even thirstier, but still we didn't get anything to drink.

In the Poltava station we again saw several lines of trains full of people being carried eastward. This time, the train standing alongside ours evidently held people from the Soviet Ukraine who were also being transported east. Apparently they were not prisoners, because their door was open and they were allowed to come out of the train, using a metal ladder by the door. Their train was standing about ten feet from ours, and we could see their faces and hear their conversations. They spoke with a typical Soviet Ukrainian accent. Their sadness and hunger were especially visible. Apart from the raggedy look of their clothing and their pale, worn faces, they lacked the sparkle of human spirit. Their traveling conditions were much better than ours. They had iron stoves in their wagons, and were probably getting their supplies of food and water more regularly than we. Still, they seemed to have lost all expression in their eyes, as if there had never been any happiness in their past lives. They were being transported from the Kharkov territory to the Omsk region in western Siberia, as we found out from their conversations. From what we could see through the small openings in our wagon, few of the women and children had shoes on. Most of the men traveling with them wore rubber galoshes. They didn't dare approach our wagon because the NKVD men were watching, and allowed no fraternization.

One woman shouted to us, "Ot kuda vih? [Where are you from?]"

"From Poland," we shouted back.

Then she said, "Why do they torment us so much? For what? We haven't harmed anybody!"

We could not carry on any further conversation. The NKVD guard appeared and she immediately went back to her train, swearing and calling him a son of a bitch and a louse. Soon our train started to move and we headed further east. We got no fuel or water until we reached the Kuybishev station, our first major stop in two days. The Kuybishev railroad station was the biggest depot we had seen up until then. Soon after the train stopped we were told by the guard to gather all our *vieschi* (belongings), as we were going to the *banya* (bath).

When we entered the bath, all our possessions were taken away from us, including the clothes we had on. Shower stalls were installed in unheated cubicles. While taking a hot shower, one stood on a cement floor on which the water was constantly freezing. The bottoms of the shower stalls were open to the cold air from outside. Everyone tried to shower as quickly as possible, even though they felt very dirty and smelly. After the shower we walked in a line into the next room to pick up our baked articles of clothing. The clothing was much too hot to touch, so we had to wait a few minutes before we could dress.

Our clothes were put into a *voshoboika* (in Russian, that literally means a louse killer), which was a special oven, like a clothes drier, available as a standard equipment at all the larger railroad stations on the Trans-Siberian railroad line. It served a very important purpose, which was killing any parasites in the clothes, such as fleas, lice, or even bedbugs, in case anybody had taken some with him from the prison cell. Many of us had them. The clothes were scorched by the heat generated in those ovens and all the little bugs got baked alive.

While we were showering, our "guardians" had prepared a rather nasty surprise for us. Two guards and a female nurse suddenly appeared at the entrance through which we were coming out of the shower. We were subjected to a very thorough personal search of all body orifices, including the anus. They seemed to be looking for something specific, but I didn't know what type of contraband they were looking for.

When the NKVD officer standing inside the exit from the bath saw me, he looked at me curiously and intently. Then he told me to come with him. I had no idea what he might have wanted of me, but I knew it was nothing to rejoice about. Another officer went along with us, armed with a submachine gun. They led me towards the rear of the train, where the NKVD guards had a special car which served as their headquarters. When I was inside their office, a *politruk* (who was responsible for the political indoctrination of prisoners) immediately called me over to his desk and very sternly asked, "What did you use to shave your face?"

I was dumbfounded. I had not yet needed to shave. I didn't have any hair growing on my face at the age of sixteen. So I answered, "I've never shaved my face."

"You're a liar! You're a damned fascist liar!" they shouted.

Then I felt a heavy blow on the side of my head that nearly knocked me unconscious. I told the politruk that I was too young to have any hair on my face, but he didn't believe me. They searched me thoroughly and took me back to the bath, sore from the blows. I was brought back to our boxcar, which had also been completely searched, but of course they hadn't found anything suspicious, such as a knife or a razor.

Three weeks had passed, and soon we approached the Ural Mountains. The blizzards and snowdrifts were so bad that our "Ark of Suffering" was forced to halt for a day or two at a time, waiting to be rescued by special snow plows. Prisoners from some of the boxcars were also enlisted to help clear the way for the train. Usually the prisoners in the forward sections of the train, closest to the mounds of snow, were called out to help.

We had gone through several periods of hunger, lack of water for two or three days at a time, and lack of fuel, coal, or wood to burn in the barrel stove. People were emaciated, cold, and hopelessly resigned. We counted days by scratching marks on the wall of the carriage. By occasionally seeing the names on the station signs we were able to orient ourselves. After Kuybishev, we passed Ufa and Chelyabinsk, which were known to all of us before this only as names on a map, somewhere in western Siberia.

Despite being exhausted and weak from starvation and cramped conditions on the wooden planks in the car, with the approach of Christmas, men began talking about various delicacies and scrumptious meals they had had in their homes in Poland. One man would start describing a deliciously roasted duck, served with gravy, baked potatoes, vegetables, and all the wonderful trimmings. Other men talked about exotic foods they had had in restaurants in Warsaw. Each would delight his listeners, and it helped to pass the time, and to forget, temporarily at least, the inhuman conditions of our reality.

Certain traditions strengthen the bonds between members of national or religious groups. One such tradition among Polish people is the *oplatek* (wafer) ritual at Christmastime, a tradition that goes back several centuries. Folklore has it that this custom was fashioned on the example of the Last Supper, when Jesus broke the bread with his disciples to teach them charity and love for one another. It was supposedly adopted in Poland by its first ruler, Prince Mieszko I (963–992), when he accepted Christianity for his nation in the tenth century. At dusk on Christmas Eve the children would watch for the first star to appear in the sky. When they announced that they had seen the star, the eldest person present or the head of the family started the ceremony. Putting all bad feelings aside, a friendly hand was extended to one another, with a piece of wafer and a hug. Best wishes and hopes were expressed for the fulfillment of one's most personal dreams. The wafers are usually made of unleavened dough and blessed by a priest in church or by one who visits homes to bless holiday wafers and other food. This ceremony before Christmas Eve dinner creates a strong feeling of solidarity and affection.

Our little group in the train shared feelings and dreams, and on that night we reassured each other that no one among us was alone. Since the rations of bread, our main sustenance, were not issued to us daily, we had to improvise. Instead of the traditional *oplatek*, we used crumbs of stale bread, which some prisoners had squirreled away for this purpose. In our thoughts we were with our loved ones and wishing each other "the fulfillment of our most private wishes." Our wishes inevitably included that God might let us survive these hellish conditions. Some of us needed to tell the story to the world outside this sinister system. Many men cried bitter tears at being so completely helpless in the struggle against evil. Others prayed for quick death to bring relief from that hell.

At the Chelyabinsk station our prison train was shunted to a side rail and we were ordered to get out with all of our possessions. *Banya* and *voshoboika* (the delousing oven) meant a chance to shed a few hungry lice from our person and our clothes.

The journey eastward, past Chelyabinsk, was rather uneventful. We had all been exhausted by hunger, thirst, cold, and sleeplessness, to the point of numbness of the spirit as well as the body. Our train didn't stop many times, and when it did it was mostly in the middle of dense taiga forest. I recall very few of the station names. Names like Omsk, Novosibirsk, Tomsk, and Krasnoyarsk I recall because I saw the big station signs in Russian characters. Other than that, the stations had no distinguishing features. The crowds looked the same—people wrapped up in black or dark gray winter clothes, with feet usually clad in felt boots, reinforced with layers of rags for warmth. The commissar in charge of the whole transport would usually stop our train in the middle of the wild country. There were fewer people around in such places. The Soviets still tried to maintain these massive transports of slaves across the continent in strict secrecy, even from their own citizens.

If our train happened to be driven into a regular railroad station, it was always shunted off onto a side track. Naturally, we were never allowed to get out, so it didn't much matter where the train stopped. Nothing mattered except one thing—getting our food! Our feeding was very irregular, and sometimes we got no water for two to four days at a time. Supply stations must have been 350 to 700 miles apart, and when the train was stopped by severe snowstorms we were stranded in the middle of nowhere. We could see only the tops of the trees buried deep in the snow. When the train was in the station we shouted in unison, *"Khleba daitie!"* or, *"Vodyh daitie!"* ("Give us bread!" or "Give us water!") The guards didn't pay much attention to our shouting, because they had orders to ignore it.

One unforgettably beautiful experience was when the train passed the southern tip of Lake Baikal. The sun was setting as we approached the lake, and for several hours we circled its southern tip. The rays of the setting sun played on the many layers of the heavy clouds hanging over the lake, creating kaleidoscopic multicolor effects. We were very close to the shoreline, perhaps seventy-five to one hundred yards from it. It was as if nature was treating us to an enchanting show to make our miserable lot a little easier to bear. We saw the city of Irkutsk only through the cracks between the boards in the side of our boxcar. We had been riding on that train about five weeks by then, under the most inhumane conditions imaginable, so our sensibilities to the misery surrounding us were deadened. Physically, we were still alive, but just barely.

We finally arrived at Komsomolsk on January 16, 1941. This was apparently our destination, although we hadn't known about it during the journey. Our journey had taken over six full weeks.

The guards opened the heavy doors and shouted, "Sobieraitie vsie svoi veshchi, da prigotovties' vihodit'! [Take all your things and prepare to disembark!]"

Our train was on a siding perhaps half a mile from the station. We were hungry, cold and exhausted, but somehow when the sliding door was opened, it felt good to look outside and breathe fresh air. The air in the train wagon was putrid from human excrement, since the *parasha* (the pail used for a toilet) was overflowing. It is said that sometimes a change is as good as a rest, and this change was very welcome indeed. We didn't know what was awaiting us!

We were let out one wagon at a time and ordered into formations of five in a row. This was the general method of marching prisoners, since it was the easiest way to keep track of their number. We stepped out into a subarctic winter air. There was a lot of snow on the ground, and our breaths formed small puffs of white mist that froze in mid-air almost instantly. We waited until a company of one hundred men was formed. Then a guard with a submachine gun announced loudly, "You are going to march to your barracks now. Remember, you must not leave your column. If you make one step to the left or right, or fall behind, we will shoot you on the spot without warning. *Ponimayete?* [Do you understand?]"

By this time we understood that they meant what they said, because we had witnessed several shootings on the way. With one guard on each side, one at the front setting the quick pace of the march, and two guards with bayonet-tipped rifles at the rear, our column of twenty rows of men, five in each row, marched for about an hour. At last we were led through a huge wooden gate covered on both sides with a double net of barbed wire. There was a watchtower with a square hut on top. A soldier with a heavy machine gun mounted on a turret was positioned so that he could immediately stop a rebellion with his gunfire. His field of vision was a perfect 360 degrees. Six other watchtowers were around a rectangular compound, which measured about a mile in length and three-quarters of a mile in width. The country around the camp was hilly and tireless except for some small, dried-up bushes. Vegetation does not grow well in such a cold, forbidding climate.

Our company was directed to occupy half of a big log house built by former groups of prisoners. Entering the door, I noticed the simple plan of the barracks—on both sides of the one-room hall, two levels of wooden planks were separated by about ten yards. There was a huge cast-iron stove and a crude wooden bench on two tree stumps. The wooden planks were for us to sleep on, but no mattresses were provided. Comfort and well-being were not given a very high priority.

It didn't take us much time to get organized, since we didn't have any personal belongings except for the few things we carried. We had gone through many searches and the guards simply took anything they liked, which left us with almost nothing.

We each picked a place on the shelves. I went up to the top shelf. Next to me was Zenon K. He was the only other member of the group from Lutsk who was with me. The rest had been separated and sent to parts unknown to us. Zenon was about three years older than I. He was not actually in our group; he was one of the liaisons between the adult underground resistance groups and the youth groups. He had been given a sentence of ten years, even though no anti-Soviet activities were proven against him and he had admitted to nothing. He was sentenced for political crimes. Now we marched together and gave each other all the spiritual or physical support we could muster when one of us showed signs of needing to lean—sometimes literally—on someone.

Two hours after we settled in the barracks, we were called to the mess hall for a meal. It had been more than a day since we had eaten anything. In the mess hall we were given a slice of bread and a plate of soup made with salted fish, some pieces of cabbage, and, if you were lucky, several grains of barley. The soup's main appeal was that it was hot, because we were still bitterly cold.

We were dead tired and didn't undress for the night. There were no pillows and no blankets to cover ourselves with. We just had to make the best of what we had with us. We even managed to joke about it, saying that each of us had three coats, one for covering ourselves with, one to spread underneath for a mattress, and one to use for a pillow. In fact it was, of course, one coat that had to be used for all three functions. I considered myself especially lucky to have my uncle Hieronim's goatskin jacket. It helped a lot to protect me from freezing right into unconsciousness.

The first night in the barrack showed me what I was going to suffer from in all the camps I would be in: bugs, particularly bedbugs. As soon as the stove heated the air in the barracks, those little bastards started bombarding us from the ceiling of the hall. They discovered my good tasting, pure blood and insisted on making a feast of me all night. I was in actual pain from their bites. They apparently didn't like Zenon's or my other neighbor's blood, because I saw them land on both of them and just slide off without biting. A second after they fell on me I felt a very slight pricking and the bug would start blowing up until he was like a droplet of blood, ruby-colored, almost transparent. Each bite meant an itching lump. When the bug was completely filled with my blood it became too heavy to hold onto my skin with its stinger and it rolled off and died. They were beastly bloodsuckers. I learned to recognize the smell of those bugs quickly—it was that of almonds.

The day after our arrival, the transit camp authorites held an auction for the men in our group. There was literally an auction block set up where men were brought to the front of a large room and representatives from large labor camps in the area checked them for their physical appearance, testing their muscles and, in some instances, looking at their teeth to see if they were good labor material. The *pom po trudu* (labor camp commander's assistants in charge of labor supply) needed to fulfill the quotas set by the regional project commission and apparently had standing contracts with the NKVD to keep their camps supplied with many thousands of fresh laborers each year. The annual mortality rate in these camps was very high, caused as much by natural causes as by indiscriminate shooting. Shooting was a sanction that was very lightly considered and often applied to the prisoners. The basic attitude of the authorities to a prisoner's life was always that it was expendable. Shooting was also used as a method of intimidation, a reminder that if a prisoner didn't like anything about his fate and wanted to challenge it, the guard's response would be swift and final.

8

Camp Bureya 2—
Can Anyone Survive?

Zenon and I were again picked for the same camp. The next day we were loaded onto trucks and off we were, on a bumpy and rough journey, in the northerly direction. We traveled about fifteen to twenty hours. There was a camp near the Bureya River (a tributary of the Amur River), where we were unloaded and again ordered to form rows of five men, twenty rows per column. Three guards were in charge of this column—the front guard had a submachine gun, one guard on the side and one at the rear. Each of these two had a bayonet-tipped heavy rifle.

The front guard was apparently the leader of this convoy, because he ran out in front and announced loud, so all could hear, "Any man who makes one step left or right out of line, or falls behind a step, will be shot without warning. *Ponimayete?* [Do you understand?]"

We stood silently, as there was nothing we could say or do. We knew the rules.

He waited a few moments, so that his message had enough time to sink into our minds. Then he shouted the next order:

"*V pierod!* [Forward march!]"

We were exhausted and totally resigned. It made no difference to us anymore what was going to happen. We were completely at their mercy. All such orders and instructions were well coded in our subconsciousness, and we all knew what would happen to anyone who dared to step out of the ranks.

The column started marching right away. We were ordered to march because the truck could not travel through that terrain after the recent snowfall. There was no road, just a path made by previous groups of prisoners who had marched through there recently. We were marching through hills and valleys with no trees, only very scanty, dry tundra bushes. The temperature was about fifty degrees below zero Fahrenheit; we could sense that with our noses, which kept freezing on us. Frost even accumulated on our chins. We had been issued winter jackets with cotton linings and warm hats, but these were not adequate protection for the viciously biting frost. We were constantly busy rubbing our faces and noses, which helped a little to stave off frostbite.

Besides the "free" guards (NKVD men), there were two or three prisoner guards from among the more senior prisoners. These men still had a little compassion for their fellow prisoners. After two or three hours of this march, when the men's endurance began to wane and some were slowing down, one of the prisoner-guards spoke to an NKVD man with a submachine gun about letting the weakened men slacken off a little and walk behind. The NKVD man's answer was quick. "If anyone feels tired or bored with life, let him fall behind."

The prisoner-guard knew exactly what would happen to a man who fell behind, no matter how little, and asked the other prisoners to hold up the weak men, to help them stay alive.

Later we did lose two men. They were exhausted and had a problem breathing. At a certain point they stumbled and fell, and before anybody could help them, one NKVD man ran toward them and shot them twice, very sternly ordering the rest of us to march on. We somehow managed to finish the march, which lasted a total of ten hours.

Marching across valleys, hills, snow drifts, rocks, and rough terrain was exhausting. We all heaved a deep sigh of relief when we finally saw a clearing in the middle of the rocky desolate country with some barracks in it. Even the guards seemed glad to see a break nearby, because they too were tired and anxious to unload their human cargo.

The authorities didn't ask any questions about the two men who were shot during the march. The guards hadn't bothered to check their names. No personal records were kept; the accounting for the prisoners was kept only in numbers. Those who fell down would simply be reported as having tried to escape. Nobody questioned the circumstances or the need for shooting them.

An important part of the purpose for establishing the rehabilitational or re-educational camps is the elimination of citizens whose attitude and behavior are thought to be threatening the position of absolute control over the people that each successive Central Committee of the Communist Party is determined to maintain. Another reason is that these millions of slave laborers work for the minimal total cost of maintenance of their lives, at the subsistence level. These slaves are changing the characteristics of millions of square miles of Russian territories, extracting untold wealth from mother earth, creating hundreds of new industries, and building hundreds of new cities. The human cost of these undertakings does not matter at all. The Russians have never really accepted Western humanistic ethics when dealing with people. One formerly high-ranking party member once, when asked about his reaction to the ruthless, bestial treatment of people in the Soviet system, answered without hesitation, as if it were a matter of no importance, "We don't know how to react to human sentiments. Our hands are all messed up to the elbows with human blood and shit."

Upon arrival we were ordered to occupy the barrack closest to the gate. We were so exhausted we could barely lift ourselves up to the wooden shelves, which were to be our beds for the next few months. For our empty, shriveled bellies we were again given the same watery soup, called *balanda*, made with salty little sardines and bits of cabbage leaves. One slice of dark rye bread was issued with the bowl of soup. This meal partially filled our stomachs, but it did not satisfy our hunger or relieve our fatigue. Fortunately, however, we were soon sound asleep.

On the morning of the first full day at our new location we were awakened at dawn. The commandant ordered a general meeting outside in the yard, even though the temperature must have been at least minus twenty degrees Fahrenheit below zero. They did this to show us right away that the temperature in the project territory would not stand in the way of normal production levels. This was a new camp, established shortly before our arrival.

The *politruk* gave us a short pep talk in a big yard between the barracks. He assumed a friendly tone and said, "Zdrastfuytie [greetings to all of you]. You have arrived here to help us with a very important task. Your job in this camp will be to build railroad tracks needed to win the war effort against the fascists who have invaded the Soviet people's fatherland.

"You will be rewarded for good efforts," said the *politruk*, "with both good care and good food. Those who are caught in any acts of sabotage will be destroyed immediately."

Listening to this speech, we all thought of our own

beloved Poland, the land of our forefathers, whose ancient homes were first so brutally attacked by the Nazis. Now they were being murderously plundered by the barbarians from the east. Many angry, furious thoughts crowded through our minds, seeming ready to explode at any moment. Our chests heaved in helpless fury. Some men lying on their dirty rags at night, completely exhausted and deadbeat, talked to themselves in desperation about often having the urge to throw themselves at "those bastard murderers" to "end their own suffering." Many of them were contemplating suicide. That kind of action would certainly bring them a quick end. Yet, to most people, life was still worth living because they had hope and faith that they would get out of there some day. I, too, had hope. We couldn't do much else in that situation besides stand there silently, meekly, in the wretched cold. We dared not open our mouths. We just listened to this murderer's lecture on patriotism towards the Great Communist Mother Russia. Alas, in order to survive, despite our deep internal resentment and revolt, we had to build a defense system for our Moscovite "friends." We had to do what they told us to do, under the constant threat of rifle barrels and bayonets directed at us. This politruk was a free man, which meant he was a member of the NKVD staff. His job was to tell us Soviet propaganda, and intimidate us into following their orders—or else!

Next spoke the *pompotrudu* (assistant camp commandant in charge of the labor force in the camp). He was a prisoner himself, who had served about ten years in labor camps and had distinguished himself as a loyal, tough survivor of the system. He had thus earned the right to be given a light, responsible job, and belonged to the camp management elite. He had been a "common," or a "social," criminal, which meant a thief, a murderer, or a person caught in a nonpolitical crime without getting inveigled in any political charges in the course of investigations and trial. He had served almost his entire sentence, and had gotten used to the camp life, especially after earning a position of authority and the right to live in separate quarters outside of the barbed-wire fence. He had begun to regard camp life as safer and better than life on the outside.

Here he had a position of power and authority, which he probably would never have earned outside in the free world.

Dimitri Petrovich Efimov spoke simply. He was not concerned about politics and patriotism. "Slushaytie [listen]," he said, "since this is a new camp, not yet fully established, we need various specialists, particularly people who could work in the *kantora* [camp office]. Specifically, now, two men are needed for this job, who are able to read and write Russian fluently."

From what I had found out about work assignments we would have here, I knew I could never compete with the adults out on the production track, digging dirt with a pick and shovel and carting it 150–200 yards. So I quickly volunteered for the office job. I raised my small hand and said:

"Ya umieyu pisat' y chitat' pa ruski [I can write and read Russian]."

As soon I as spoke, the *politruk* acknowledged my application. I noticed many heads turn towards me, but I didn't see friendly expressions in their faces. I think most of the men resented the fact that I might be getting into a soft job.

After the meeting was over, the *pompotrudu* told me to come with him to the office. There, he told me to write my name in Russian and tell him briefly, in Russian, what kind of education I had had. That was easy. I just mentioned the level of schooling I had reached and that I could read, write and speak in the Polish and Ukrainian languages, in addition to Russian. He congratulated me, saying, "Vot, synok' [well, sonny], we need people like you here. You will help us organize the files and administration, to keep records on the production in this camp."

Along with me, he chose a young Russian prisoner about three years older than I. His name was Aleksei Ivanovich Tishkin, Alyosha for short. Alyosha and I became friends instantly. It is said that one can see the reflection of another person's soul deep in his eyes. It is as if one man's psychic transmission waves are suddenly attracted, received, and accepted by the other person's receiving apparatus. Something clicked between us at the first sight and we became "soul" friends right away.

Alyosha told me his story in several installments. He was raised in the Kuybishev region, near the Volga River. He had completed his ten-year comprehensive school program in 1939. His pals in his graduating class had been organizing a party, and each person was to bring whatever item was in easiest reach. Everyone tried their best to get what they could. Their possibilities were quite limited, since even essentials were usually unavailable. Alyosha told me that his people had to stand in line for hours, even in the best of times, before the war. Starting in the evening, members of each family would take turns standing in lines in front of various retail stores, to get food items or other goods. When I told Alyosha that we could buy practically anything we wanted without queueing up, he simply could not believe me. He said I was telling him propaganda.

Alyosha's aunt worked in the local Soviet restaurant, so his part for the graduation party was to try to get some food and drink. But Mother Fortune had turned against

Alyosha. He was caught red-handed at night, carrying a packet of sausage and a cake out the back door of the restaurant.

He was arrested instantly, without being given a chance to explain his actions. Later, when he mentioned that it wasn't really for him, but for a school party, it made matters much worse for him. His act was called conspiracy, for the purpose of defrauding the honest, hard-working people of the local Soviet council. After the whole group of students was thoroughly investigated and put to trial by the local Soviet's judge, three of the teenagers were sentenced to five years of hard labor in re-educational camps.

Thus Alyosha's practical life education was to continue in the prison camps. He learned the truth about the inner workings of the whole Soviet society, once he was put outside of it, in a camp for the undesirables. We talked a lot about each other's life circumstances, experiences, and dreams. I told Alyosha about my activities, my friends, the organizations I had belonged to, my church work, and how happy I was as a child.

Alyosha's family consisted of his parents, his brother Michael (Misha they called him), and his sister Tatyana (Tasha). His mother's parents also lived with them. They all loved *Dyedushka* (Grandpa), who used to tell them lovely stories about his youth under the tsarist regime. His grandfather's family was very religious. With great nostalgia the grandfather would tell about the deep devotion and reverence expressed by his whole family toward Christ and His Mother.

My Russian friend told me about those stories as we worked in the *kantora*, setting up files for the prisoners. We told each other about various incidents from our life before being arrested. We even visited each other's barracks so we could quietly spend more time together. My experiences during my youth, up to the age of sixteen, had been rich and unique enough to warrant sharing them with Alyosha.

I told him about the boy scouts, camping, and the trips we took, about the national and church holiday celebrations, and the sport games among our unorganized teams. I illustrated the beauty of the surroundings of my little town of Lutsk to Alyosha, where I grew up and grew to love so much. I thought there was no lovelier place on earth than the fields and forests around Lutsk, where I roamed so freely. The town itself was charming and interesting, with the clear waters of the Styr River winding through the middle of it. And, of course, there was also the medieval castle and the cathedral, where the ghosts of the ancient heros and villains "spoke" to us on several occasions.

As I told those stories of my past to Alyosha, I realized at the same time that those happy years had gone by irretrievably.

Reliving those past years by sharing them with my soul friend strengthened my own spirits and fortified my stubborn will and resolve to fight my own weaknesses in order to survive. Among my weaknesses that I tried to eliminate was one that I thought was the most dangerous—the urge to give in to my tiredness and collapse suddenly. No matter how tired I was, I always tried to go on and do what I had to to preserve my good health. It made me want so much more to last through it all and to return, when all the bad was over, to my beloved town. Every day I drew new strength from the fountain of my memories. I also thought about how poor those people are who have no memories of happy times in their hearts. Alyosha often had tears in his eyes when he told me about his family life and how strange and confused he felt many times during the politruk's lectures and *Komsomol* activities. The Komsomol was the communist youth's equivalent of the boy scouts. The "Scripture" and the "sermons" in the Komsomol meetings were the teachings of Marx and Engels. The main tenets of those teachings were: 1) that the State and the Party were the supreme authorities, and 2) that young Komsomol's loyalty was, first and last, to the party, and not to one's parents or family. Alyosha loved his family dearly, including his grandparents, and could never reconcile within himself the teachings of the Komsomol politruks or other zealots.

He was particularly interested in my stories about my work as an altar boy in the church. There was a *pravoslavny* (Greek Orthodox) church in his town, and Alyosha's grandfather took him along to many church services. He was thrilled by the deep emotions awakened in him during the unforgettable choir-singing, the processionals, and many Sunday and holiday services. For at least a few weeks our emotions soared to high levels together.

We both wanted to meet again after our sentences were finished, although Alyosha sadly predicted that it couldn't be, because some more experienced prisoners had told him that it almost never happened that a prisoner is released and allowed to live a normal civilian life, after having served a term in the prison camps. He could never be a normal citizen again, because he had seen the truth about the Great Soviet Motherland.

His predictions soon became reality. The *politruk* looked into my folder during a routine inspection of prisoners' files in the office and immediately established that I was a dangerous element, having been sentenced under Article 54, Section 58. I was a counterrevolutionary, a spy of the capitalist-fascist regimes, the *politruk* had concluded. I had to be immediately removed from the influential and sensitive office job and put outside, on the production line. So my soft job lasted only about two months.

The next day I was awakened before dawn, along with the rest of the brigade. Morning reveille was made by the assistant commandant in charge of work brigades—he banged on a piece of rail with an iron rod. The first rousing call was made about 4:00 A.M. At the same time, a guard appeared in the door, making a frightful noise with his shouting, which sounded as if we were being attacked by Martians (although maybe that wouldn't have been as abominable as our reality). He meant business, and he had a big stick in his hand.

I had just shaken the last bug off and was still scratching my lumpy back when my friend Zenon K. pulled me into his brigade. They had recently lost two of their men due to an "accident." After eating breakfast we put on our warmest clothes, because the temperature was below zero. We had been issued cotton-stuffed jackets and trousers, a reasonably warm winter hat with ear flaps, and felt boots, which were okay as long as they didn't get wet. Before we left the barracks we had to drink a mugful of a special brew called *khwoya* out of a barrel standing next to the exit door. This drink was made by boiling the needles of a cedar tree, which grew locally. The drink was as bitter as wormwood, but they warned us to drink a mugful every morning as a preventive measure against scurvy. We didn't mind having to drink this bitter medicine because we all knew that scurvy was a dreaded disease. I still don't know if it is a deterrent against scurvy, or even if it has any Vitamin C in it. I did see several people with scurvy symptoms, *e.g.*, loosening teeth, sore gums, and in its later stages, sores over the entire body.

Soon I was to see a dying man in the final stages of scurvy. It was a horrible, unforgettable sight. This man was Grisha Petrov, a Russian political prisoner about thirty-five to forty years old, with about ten years in the prison-camp system. He had sores all over his body and was often short of breath. Whenever he stood up, a progressively thickening ridge was visible in an even line around his waist. His body had not been able to dispose of liquids for some time, and the condition had worsened soon after I met him in the barrack. The ridge climbed progressively higher, and as it reached closer and closer to the level of his heart, he felt a tighter and tighter choking sensation. One day, right after we got back from work late at night, Grisha Petrov went into choking convulsions and thrashed about on the bare wooden floor while two men tried to restrain him so that he wouldn't hurt himself. He was a big man, and was now finding it difficult to breathe. His breathing sounded like a terrible kind of snoring, except that we all knew he wouldn't wake up from this condition. He expired that night. He was buried in the snow outside the camp's fence, because the ground was frozen.

Our work area was about three miles away from the camp enclosure. It was a wild, hilly area, and we were preparing the ground for a railroad. Hills had to be dynamited and broken up, and depressions in the land had to be filled. On my first day at work my heart sank as I saw that I wouldn't be able to fulfill the established work quota. The job was to use a pick to break up huge chunks of frozen dirt (often with rocks in it, dynamited from a huge hill), then use a shovel to load it into the wheelbarrow. The loaded wheelbarrow had to be balanced carefully and pushed on wooden planks for about 250 yards, and then dumped into deep holes and depressions in the ground to even out the terrain.

The overall plan for the prisoners in the hundreds of camps in the area was to build a railroad that would run parallel to the Trans-Siberian railroad built several decades before. There was great fear of a Japanese attack on the far eastern reaches of the USSR. The Japanese had taken over Manchuria, and the only Soviet railroad connecting the eastern port of Vladivostok with central and European Russia was the single-line railroad from Vladivostok to Moscow. Our line was to run about 800 to a thousand miles north of the original line.

Another generation of Polish slave workers, under the tsarist regime, had been used in the construction of the original railroad line, back in the nineteenth century. Thousands of Polish political prisoners, who fought to regain Poland's freedom, were arrested by the tsarist troops and marched to Siberia to work there on railroad construction gangs. These men (and some women) had fought in the uprising of 1863, which the tsarist troops had brutally put down. Vignettes of several generations of Polish martyrs who fought bravely to throw off the yoke of slavery imposed upon Poland by the previous Russian regime had flashed through our minds, but at the time we could do nothing but face the immediate grim reality.

I took a few half-filled wheelbarrows on the first day and received a few strikes from the brigadier's steel rod for being too slow. He thought I was just being lazy. On the second and third days I did a little better, but not much. The brigadier whipped me again, but at the end of the week he began to see that I just couldn't measure up to the task.

I saw other, much more powerful men being beaten viciously with the steel rod for slowing down their pace.

The brigadier actually wanted men to run with the empty wheelbarrows when going back uphill for the next load. Some men tried to even exceed the quota so that they could get *Stakhanovich* premiums, which meant that they would receive up to twice the normal ration of four hundred grams of bread daily, and soups richer with fat for their meals. They were also praised and proudly shown off by the pompotrudu during daily inspection, while the P.A. systems blasted patriotic Soviet songs over the entire camp. Ultimately, however, it did them no good, because after a few months of such intensive strain these strong men were finished; their muscles were simply overworked. Without substantial nourishment, their torn muscles wouldn't heal, and they developed hernias and other physical ailments. Whole brigades, famished and exhausted by the excessive hard work in the subzero temperatures, tried heroically to meet the quotas, but simply faded away. As a brigade's output kept falling, so its rations went down. The administration wanted more output, so they ordered longer work days, up to sixteen hours a day. The brigades were ordered to go to work in temperatures down to fifty degrees below zero.

The temperature around the work area, stayed, on the average, between twenty and forty degrees below zero throughout January, February, and March. The frosty air seemed to smite exposed skin like a whip, and the tips of our noses and ears had to be constantly rubbed to prevent severe frostbite.

One day we were not driven out of our barrracks to work, because the temperature had dropped to below minus forty degrees. That day I went out to chop some thick tree stumps that were dumped near our barrack for firewood. I was surprised to see how very easy it was to chop two- to three-foot thick stumps with a light blow of the ax. The wood was so brittle from the extremely low temperatures that merely dropping the ax from above my head split the stump apart. I went over to the alcohol thermometer on the side of another barrack. I couldn't believe my eyes—the temperature reading showed forty degrees below zero. Instinctively, I felt myself to make sure I was still alive and able to stand. In spite of, or perhaps because of the extreme cold, the air seemed very fresh and clean. It would have indeed been a healthy environment, if one were fed enough to compensate for the fast loss of body heat. When I urinated outside, the urine didn't make a hole in the snow, but froze instantly into strange-looking figurines.

What made it much easier to bear these extremely low temperatures was the fact that there was no wind. The white smoke rose from the barrack chimney in a perfect pillar, rising undisturbed by any air currents. The skies above were light blue and cloudless.

Fortunately for me, my brigadier took pity on me and arranged with the administration to assign me to a new job. I was given a notebook and a pencil and told to stand on a hill above the tracks and count the number of loads delivered daily by all prisoners in the brigade.

My friend Zenon K. was still in the same brigade with me. By a stroke of good luck the camp also had a Polish prisoner doctor, Dr. Edmund Karski, who had declared himself to be a heart specialist. Dr. Karski saved many lives among the Polish prisoners, including my own and Zenon's. When he recorded the results of a physical examination, he stated, among other things, that Zenon K. had heart murmurs and that he was unfit for heavy physical exertion. Since the camp administration had developed a very respectful attitude toward Dr. Karski, his professional opinions were taken seriously. Dr. Karski also provided medical services to the administrative personnel and the NKVD, including their wives. In that manner he developed good, friendly relationships with the guards and the office personnel.

Both Zenon and I greatly benefited from the good advice and services of Dr. Karski. Indeed, it wasn't just wise advice, because the good doctor many times gave us cod-liver oil and other medicinal foods, to which he had access. Those foods at least partially made up for the lack of fat in our diet, and most importantly, vitamins A and E.

While standing on the hill, counting the loads of dirt delivered, I had a chance to help those whom I could trust without fear of being reported. Every so often, several times a day, I recorded for Zenon and some of the other men an official count substantially higher than their own actual count. That meant that they would get better and more food, which helped them to keep up their strength and survive longer.

Days and weeks were passing by. Most days were exactly alike, just routine happenings, with certain functions performed on a daily basis. Daily cycle was determined by the camp's higher powers. It was hard to distinguish one day from another. And yet, every so often, certain unforgettable events occurred which made us remember them. They even seemed unbelievable, but they were, nevertheless, authentically true. One such incident, although it did not just happen once, persists in my mind.

From my elevated position on the hill I had a good view of the whole work area. I saw many vicious beatings with the steel rod that the brigadiers used to get more work out of the poor wretches. The guards, armed with submachine guns, stood higher up than I and oversaw everyone. Once, a man who had just delivered a load and was coming uphill with an empty wheelbarrow had asked the guard to allow him to go off to the side to attend to his biological needs, to which the guard consented. The man was about forty yards from where I stood. After fifteen to twenty minutes passed, the man started to get up and fix his clothes to go back to work. Just as he took his first steps the guard aimed his machine gun and shot him dead. The guard later reported that the prisoner had tried to escape. When I first saw this vicious, murderous treatment of weak, defenseless people, and the beatings and shootings, I couldn't look. I winced, and was horrified, my knees shook, and I almost vomited several times.

Witnessing this sight and several others like it has been eating on my consciousness ever since then. It put an indelible impression on my mind as to how little a man's life was worth to this band of murderers. It was extremely hard for me to control the fear and panic that this senseless, vain murder evoked in me. I wanted to scream and run, but deep sorrow and pity for the man who was so unreasonably and unnecessarily stricken dead made it impossible for me to issue a sound. My weak legs shook and wouldn't move from the spot. Several prisoners saw this wanton killing, but not one reacted. I saw then that my violent reaction to this brutality could only be used against me.

I realized that I would be risking my life by reacting so strongly. The guards couldn't tolerate any show of emotion or sentimentality. I just had to get used to it and learn not to react at all. In order to survive in those camps a man had to learn certain rules of behavior. First of all, he had to learn to make a good effort to never refuse any order given to him by the guard, no matter how cruel or preposterous. A prisoner always had to show proper humility and fear of the guard.

Officially the guards had no right to destroy the weakest men. We were never secure, however, for our lives always depended to a great extent on the whims of the guards. They had an absolute authority over us, and most of them were sick with hatred and fear of the "fascists," whoever that meant. They shot at the prisoners for entertainment or personal pleasure and satisfaction, just like a hunter shoots at a wild duck. In many cases a man's only crime was that he was a member of a brigade that frequently had not fulfilled its quota of work, either because it had been set unrealistically high or because the brigade's members were weakened by a long period of malnutrition. Penalty for such crimes was either mass shootings, or a reduction in rations for the entire brigade. This led to the inevitable destruction of all members of the brigade.

One day we heard that a prisoner had escaped. We wondered how and where a man could escape from that camp. It was at least seven to eight hundred miles to the Manchurian border, and the closest free human settlement was no less than two hundred miles away. The terrain was visible and covered with snow most of the time, making it virtually impossible for a man to camouflage himself successfully. In any event, two days later we had to view what remained of the escapee. He was tied to the gate in a standing position, because he could not stand up on his own strength. He was almost blinded and had had most of his clothes torn up, and his skin had been ripped apart by the dogs. The guards made us pause by the gate so that we could have a good look at the poor, wretched victim. The man was giving up the ghost, and yes, it made a very strong impression on us. Ironically, the P.A. system blasted out a Red Army song at full strength:

Shiroka strana moya radnaya,
Mnogo v niey lesov, poley y rek,
Ya drugoy takoy stranyh nye znayu,
Gdye tak volno dyshyt' chelovyek.

Oh, how great is my native country,
With its many forests and lakes,
I know not any other land
Wherein a man can breathe so freely.

While I was working as an *otmyetchik* (counter of loads), I witnessed three more cases of the extreme inhumanity and cruelty of the guards. Men exhausted beyond the point of endurance actually broke down under the weight and the sway of the loaded wheelbarrows as they pushed them down the 250-yard wooden gangway. The gangway planks were precariously perched upon posts some thirty or forty feet above the bottom of the ravine, which was being filled up to ground level. In three separate incidents a man was going down the gangway with his wheelbarrow full of dirt when the gangway began to shake. Each man was insecure on his feet from fatigue and from the extended period of starvation. One man lost his balance, the load tipped to one side, and it simply pulled the poor slave down into the ravine. The guard saw this, and when the man reached the bottom the guard sent a couple of well-aimed shots, which finished the man's pain from the fall. No one dared to go after the man's body; the guards wouldn't allow it. So the workers had to continue dumping their loads. The other two men apparently fell down due to a blackout or dizziness; they lost control of their empty wheelbarrows, and tumbled down off the gangway. In time the men's bodies were buried, as the ravine was leveled off. Their wheelbarrows, however, were recovered and mended for new men to use.

Once I saw a very strange-looking man pushing a fully loaded wheelbarrow down the wooden gangway. He was bigger than the average prisoner. What especially caught my attention was the appearance of his face. I couldn't see much of it under the side flaps of the big winter hat that covered most of his square face. His eyes were very squinted—he was Mongolian.

In my elevated position, as scorekeeper, I had to know all the men's names so that I could report how much each man had accomplished in a day. This strange man's given name sounded like Aboul Turkhai. He was one of millions of Asians "liberated" against their will from their problems and freedoms as nomadic people, and subsequently sovietized. Aboul was from the Soviet Republic of Turkmenia. At first I was a little afraid to approach Aboul—he looked so dangerous and hostile. I spoke to him in Russian:

"Hey, man, what's your name?"

"Why do you want to know my name?" he answered.

"I have to report the number of loads you've brought over, that's all."

He was silent for a moment; then I spoke again. "You don't need to be afraid of me. I am just a fellow prisoner—from Poland."

Aboul's face seemed to change its shape as he began to smile. When he smiled to me the change in his square-shaped face was so great that even if he didn't speak a word of Russian we would have become friends.

He was silent for the next few minutes, as if debating with himself whether I was telling the truth. Then he said, loud and proudly, in Russian, "My name is Aboul Turkhai. I am from Turkmenia."

That was what it sounded like to me, and I wrote it

that way, in Russian, on my record. His speech was much different from that of other prisoners. In our next several conversations Aboul and I were quite communicative. Aboul found it hard to pronounce certain Russian words; somehow his vocal chords would not respond easily to my tutoring, because of a lack of training. But he did know some very choice swear words for times when he wanted to refer to the Russian NKVD men, or the guards in general. He had been tortured inhumanely by NKVD investigators to make him confess what they wanted to hear, even though it was not true. Thus they would have proof of his guilt and could send him to the labor camps. After torturing Aboul and the members of his family, the NKVD resettled his family to a remote location in eastern Siberia, and Aboul himself was sentenced to ten years in a rehabilitational hard-labor camp as an enemy of the Soviet people. When I met him, he had served about four years.

Aboul had a strange-looking face; it was almost as wide at the forehead as it was by the chin. When during one of our later conversations I explained to him how I was taken away from my home and family and what my true feelings were about the Russians, the Mongol's normally gloomy and angry face brightened and a pleasant smile appeared. He also told me in a few words his burning hatred for the Russians. When he smiled, his chin widened even more, and then it was equal in width to his forehead, forming a perfect square. It was pretty much as I had imagined men from the Stone Age.

My subsequent meetings with Aboul were much friendlier from then on. I had gained his trust, and perhaps even his friendship. He would start talking to me while he was passing by, straining his powerful body under the burden of a wheelbarrow full of rocks and dirt. He also told me of his family.

Aboul was born and raised in Turkmenia, which was located in the southwestern part of Siberia, near the Iranian and Afghanistan borders. His ancient nation led mostly a nomadic style of life, since the land around them was barren and unproductive. They have been living there near the Caspian Sea since the times of Genghis Khan (1162–1227).

The Soviets forced them to join the large government-owned farms, so-called *sov-hosses*. Those who resisted were summarily rounded up and shipped away into the rehabilitational forced-labor camps. Aboul was subjected to long interrogations and tortures through which he was forced to confess to socio-political crimes he had never committed. Thus he was given a ten-year sentence, to be served in the labor camps. His family was scattered throughout the various parts of the Soviet Union, and he had no chance to make contact with them. He was filled with helpless anger and great hatred. When he used some very ill-sounding words to describe the Soviet guards and their whole system, it seemed to bring out a relieved look on his face.

Eventually, the month of May came. In the northern regions of Siberia the seasons of the year change on a different cycle. The old-timers in the labor camps said, "Winter here lasts only ten months of the year—the rest is all summer."

There was hardly a noticeable spring, or, rather, it was compressed into some two to three weeks. The deeper layers of the ground stay frozen permanently; only about two or three feet of the top layer, consisting mostly of a blanket of moss, is revived by the onset of the spring/summer season. The layer of moss serves as a very fertile soil for the special vegetation of that region. Then, almost perceptibly to the eye, grasses and shrubbery grow, with their many multicolored flowers. The nights become very short, but not very dark, and the days grow much longer. The warm winds from China and Manchuria sped up the process of awakening nature in the higher regions. The valleys stay cold longer, as the warm air doesn't enter the protected ravines and large spaces between the hills. The quick transition from the breath-freezing cold of minus forty-to-sixty degree days to plus forty-to-sixty degree warm, long days made our sixteen-hour workday a little easier to bear. It may have been an illusion, but our very existence and survival became a trifle more hopeful. My friend Zenon K. and I both occasionally visited the camp doctor, Dr. Karski, but, in general, we felt very weak from the poor nourishment and the lack of good rest for several months.

The sporadic news that filtered into the camp with the new brigades of soulless, broken-down miserables was that the great USSR *rodina* (fatherland) was being mercilessly stomped by the modern, mechanized high-stepping Germans.

9

False Freedom

At the beginning of August 1941, news came to us at the Bureya #2 Camp that German military might had attacked the Soviets and was advancing, blitzkrieg-style, deep into the USSR.

There were also rumors that the Polish citizens would be freed from prisons, labor camps, and civilian resettlement locations. All Polish citizens would be allowed to join the Polish Army, which was going to be formed in one of the southern republics of Soviet-Asian USSR.

At first we couldn't believe all this wonderful news, because we were still getting barbarous treatment from the brutal brigade commanders, who continued to wield metal rods over our backs and force us to work fourteen to sixteen hours a day.

Soon, within the first half of August, we received official orders. This news that seemed too improbable before was now being confirmed. The official orders had come through.

A few days later the *politruk*, an NKVD colonel, announced at the morning head count the names of the men who were to be taken back to the regional distribution center at Komsomolsk. The next day, at daybreak, we were roused and fed the usual breakfast of soup, a slice of bread, and a mug of khwoya. We were ordered by the *politruk* to form the usual formations of one-hundreds and then loaded onto trucks. No one could believe that we were actually being set free and allowed to join the Polish Army. The journey back to Komsomolsk was much happier than was the journey to the camp. The guards seemed less mean, less threatening than they had been to us since our arrest. We were still crowded onto the trucks so that everyone had to stand up for the duration of the ten- or eleven-hour ride. The terrain we crossed was then covered with bushes of multicolored flowers, and the ground was blanketed by a thick layer of moss in full magenta bloom. The skies were cloudless and the whole world seemed much happier. The birds were flying above and singing happily. We all were beginning to experience a rebirth of hope from the total despair and depression of only days before.

At the Komsomolsk camp we were again put in the same bug-infested barracks, but now it didn't seem to matter very much. The whole world seemed to be happier, or perhaps this was only happiness awakening within us now. The sensation of beautiful nature and sunny weather aroused the urging desire of an irrepressible longing for freedom. The fleas, lice, and bedbugs were competing with one another in jumping out of the cracks and crevices between the round logs from which the walls and the ceilings were made. But having lived through the torturous treatment of the labor camps, we all felt that we could survive the few and remaining days in this transit camp. Only a person deprived of freedom can appreciate its importance and its value.

Freedom is, without any doubt, the greatest treasure a human being can possess. Longing for lost freedom is so strong, so deeply felt, that it cannot be described. All our thoughts had a single direction, one single point on which they concentrated every minute of every hour. If it were possible to devise an apparatus to monitor our thoughts, it would certainly show that thoughts of regaining freedom (in a person who has been deprived of it) occupy all cells of our gray matter. Sometimes these thoughts of freedom were so oppressive that they would explode our minds. Men lost control of themselves for no apparent reason. This desire was the most real and strongest I have ever felt. Even the hunger for food took second place then.

It may be that the continuous passiveness in all of our actions, the ceaseless, complete, and blind subjugation in everything we did, was why our entire nervous system was worked up to such a high pitch. We, the damned martyrs of brute force and violence, had waited long for deliverance.

The next day we idly watched some fifteen to twenty thousand wretched shadows of humanity being marched from one end of the camp to the other, as other brigades were being led the other way. Men were being sorted and shuffled without any apparent reason or design. We began to hear disturbing rumors, at least disturbing for some of us. First it was said that only those who actually gave their nationality as Polish were being freed. Such news, officially unconfirmed as yet, acted upon us as the best spiritual uplift. We thought that, at last, we would get out of our shackles, and that we would soon be allowed to return to our sacred homes. Our painful longing was even more acute now, after we received the latest news. Our homeland was being mercilessly brutalized, its people were being killed by the thousand. Poland and her people were being victimized and needed its sons and daughters to continue the fight against the Nazi killers.

We were anxious to return and resume the struggle for our independence. These thoughts persecuted all of us now; we could not think about anything except going back home. The NKVD investigators persuaded many Jewish and Ukrainian prisoners that Poland had ceased to exist as a state, and that they should, for the record, give just their ethnic nationality, *i.e.*, Jewish or Ukrainian. Now these men were in despair, for the politruks, in reviewing their prison files, told them that the amnesty agreement between General Sikorski's Polish government, in exile in England, and the USSR said that only actual Polish citizens were to be set free. Having their hopes shattered was a terrible blow for those expecting to be freed. We felt sorry for all the prisoners from the Polish minority groups, who allowed themselves to be misled by the NKVD agents. What is there left for a man to live for if he has lost all hope for regaining freedom?

According to General Sikorski's agreement with Joseph Stalin, all Polish citizens were to be freed and allowed to enlist in the Polish army about to be formed in the southwestern parts of Siberia. Yet the NKVD agents throughout all territories where Polish prisoners were kept or where families were resettled, managed to cunningly twist and misconstrue the terms of the agreement, thereby depriving hundreds of thousands of our people of their freedom.

The word *amnesty* angered us terribly. By any dictionary definition this word means pardoning for rebellious deeds against the sovereign. But the Soviets were not our sovereigns, and we were convinced that what we had done in showing our resistance to the invader of our country was our sacred duty and obligation.

This was a transit camp, in which we could not stay very long. Each day new transports of prisoners arrived from various labor camps scattered throughout the vast Siberian territory. It might seem that such waiting, especially now, when we did not work and had plenty of time, would be hard and exhausting, but it wasn't. Time ran fast toward freedom.

For the next two days we were left alone. We could watch from our barrack's window as thousands of other human beings were shuffled senselessly, back and forth, from one end of the camp to another. The next day the same people seemed to be led back, the other way.

By the time our turn came up to be interviewed, other rumors, even more horrible, were being whispered: Not all the Polish prisoners were being freed. Prisoners were being further segregated according to the code article under which they had been tried and sentenced in the People's Court. We saw large sections of certain brigades being led in new groups to different barracks—they were all political prisoners. Now they were branded with the worst names, such as counterrevolutionary, enemy of the people, or dangerous elements. As such, they would not be set free, no matter what the amnesty agreement had said.

My friend Zenon K. and I were now in the category of dangerous elements. Apparently the local political commandant of the gathering distribution center at Komsomolsk decided that it was unheard of to rehabilitate people branded as dangerous elements and sentenced according to Article 54, Section 58 of the Soviet criminal code. Rehabilitation of live people rarely occurred in the history of the Soviet justice system. According to the commandant's interpretation of the communique from Moscow, amnesty was to be given only to those Polish citizens who had been sentenced for nonpolitical transgressions against the then-existing laws, i.e., for common murders, theft, and business speculations, such as profiteering or smuggling.

After my interview with the investigator I was immediately moved to a different barrack. Zenon K. was taken somewhere else. It was a crushing blow to my spirit, and my body refused to go any further. Suddenly I felt terribly weak and exhausted, feeling the ravaging effects of months of scurvy, bleeding dysentery, diarrhea, and the cruel treatment by the guards. But my "guardian angel," with whom I consulted often, urged me not to give up. I followed the orders of my inner voice like a worn-out robot.

I found myself in a group of about eighty prisoners, all in approximately the same condition as myself, on a truck headed in a northeasterly direction. We were driven for some three days through desolate tundra country. The group consisted of only Polish political prisoners, all in the most miserable state, both physically and spiritually. I wondered why they bothered taking us anywhere. We certainly were not fit for any work, so why not just end our misery? If they were not giving us the "final" treatment, maybe this was another way to freedom.

In spite of these disturbing guesses, we hoped there would be another solution, that perhaps the Soviets don't really want to destroy us. This undying hope, deep in my consciousness, allowed me to bear the sickness and many hardships of everyday existence.

We arrived at a camp called Osnovnaya. We soon learned that this was a special camp, organized to allow prisoners to die a natural death. But perhaps we were sent here to await some other solution. The rations were minimal, even for these conditions—three hundred grams of bread and a watery cabbage soup, with no visible cabbage. Within days some of our men fell victim to epidemics of bleeding dysentery, food poisoning, and pneumonia.

Starving Soviet camp thugs occasionally attacked men carrying bread rations from the local camp bakery to our clinic barracks. One day I happened to be scavenging for food scraps behind the kitchen when suddenly I heard a violent commotion in the yard. I saw a tray with a pile of bread rations fly up in the air; the whole incident could not have lasted more than a minute. The tray and slices of bread fell to the ground, and two men scuttled about, picking up the bread from the ground. They quickly disappeared, as if nothing had happened. A few men went hungry that day, without even a piece of bread to eat.

It felt a little strange being a prisoner and yet not being out to work. I spent most of my time in the clinic. Three and a half months passed rather quickly in the camp of the final solution. My time in the clinic was partly as a patient and partly as a helper. When in my own barracks I slept most of the time. I was extremely weak, to the point that I could not lift my legs to walk straight or to raise my body to the place assigned to me on the first tier of plank beds. Almost every day the orderly in the barracks found a dead body on the sleeping planks.

Whenever I felt physically capable, I spent much of the day scavenging for food scraps around the rear of the camp kitchen. Occasionally I found some potato peelings among the garbage from the kitchen. The peelings had remnants of potato on them, so I washed them carefully, took them to my barracks, and baked them on top of the cast-iron heating stove. The peels provided some fractional nourishment. Even if they didn't help much they certainly didn't harm me, for I outlasted many other men who were present for the morning head counts but dead by the end of the day.

There were other men who picked the garbage with me but couldn't wait to wash and cook the peelings—they put their findings directly in their mouths. Thus they were poisoned by rotten bits they found. Many of them died.

I believe that Someone, who watches all creatures all

the time, didn't allow my hunger to become a senseless greed. I referred to that wonderful force, that Someone, as my guardian angel.

In such circumstances, when the whole traditional system of justice and fairness was breaking apart, it seemed that the only way to survive was to invoke the supernatural forces and keep a strong faith. Such faith was firmly rooted in me.

Soon I was able to celebrate my best-ever Christmas Eve, 1941.

10
Freedom at Last!

Christmas Eve of 1941 was the most memorable for all of us who had managed to survive in the camp of *dohodiagi* ("goners" or down-and-outs). The camp *politruk* in charge of political rehabilitation, Lieutenant Stepanoff, summoned all the remaining Polish citizens in the camp for a very important message.

Only eight of us were left out of eighty men brought to this camp just slightly over three months earlier. The rest of the original group had died by natural death, as our captors reported it. The meeting was held in the *politruk*'s large office, which was equipped with seats for each of us. On the large wall behind his desk was a huge map of the USSR.

"I've called you here today," said Colonel Stepanoff, "to inform you that you have all been made citizens of the great Union of Soviet Republics."

We were not sure whether we heard correctly, or what this meant for us.

"Tovarishchy! [comrades!]" continued Colonel Stepanoff. "We received new orders from Moscow, through our regional office, that you are all to be freed as of today."

He repeated, "As of today, you are free."

We caught the word *free*—it sounded so beautiful, so unbelievably longed for. He did say "free"! It took a few moments for us to accept it. Then, instantly, we swelled with indescribable feelings of joy and limitless happiness, that, at last, it's happened! We had lived long enough to hear it spoken to us, even though there were only eight of us to celebrate this great holiday. It made little difference at the moment—we were joyful, we have survived! As if in response to a command, when we realized fully what it meant, we jumped up from the benches and started hugging and kissing each other. We were all one team now, as if we had just won a fiercely competitive game. We rejoiced, in spurts, each time more wildly. Our joy was so great, that if it could have been measured, it would have exceeded the highest peaks of the Himalayas. He had even called us *tovarishchy*!

Some showed tears in their eyes.

"You can travel wherever you want," Colonel Stepanoff said further, "but not west of the Ural Mountains."

The end of his sentence certainly dampened our joy.

We raised questions. "If we can't return home to Poland, where shall we go? Poland is far beyond the Ural Mountains!"

Colonel Stepanoff had an answer for us. He took a pointer in his hand and came close to the map on the wall. He waved with the pointer across the map, from the left side of the map to the right, i.e., from the eastern borders of Poland to the Kamchatka peninsula and the port of Vladivostok in the Far East. He then repeated a similar move with his pointer from the icebound Arctic Ocean in the North to the borders of Mongolia and Afghanistan in the South, and said with his head proudly raised, "eto vsio nasha bolshaya sovietskaya rodinah!! [This is all our great Soviet fatherland!]"

Next, turning the pointer to the South, he added, "You may go here, to the Asian sector of Siberia in the south. You will have plenty of sun, and fruits of all kinds."

He pointed to Kazakhstan and Uzbekstan, near the Afghanistan border.

When we heard the words *sun* and *fruits*, our thoughts brightened.

He further explained that there was a war raging against the Nazi invaders in the European part of the USSR and that the Soviet people needed our help in their struggle against Hitler's brutal armies. Here, in the south, we would be able to join the Polish Army—to save our own lives, we ought to go south, to the Asiatic Soviet republics. After all these arguments, we were still sad, yet we all agreed that there was no better choice for us, but to go south.

Without much discussion, we unanimously agreed to go to Samarkand, the capital of Uzbekstan.

"You will each receive money and supplies for your journey, which will take you about twenty-two days from Khabarovsk," said Colonel Stepanoff as he dismissed us.

The next morning, without any further delay, we received our money and supplies for the journey. We were given thirteen rubles per day, a total of 286 rubles.

One ruble was valued as equal to one American dollar, but the buying power of the ruble fluctuated wildly, depending on the availability of goods, which were largely unobtainable. Since the politruk predicted that we might have problems buying food on the way, due to war-caused shortages and confusion, he told us that he would give us some provisions. Each of us would get an eleven-pound loaf of bread, six-and-a-half pounds of dry, salted herring, and our choice of either six-and-a-half pounds of sauerkraut or a like quantity of dry onions. I chose the onions.

After receiving these healthful victuals, we wasted no time in getting ourselves ready for the journey back into the dangerous, challenging world of the free people. Toward evening one member of our group, a little fellow by the name of Eddie, came to the rest of us, alarmed and crying, saying that some Russian hoodlums in the camp beat him up and robbed him of all his money. We immediately held a counsel and unanimously decided that Eddie would continue with us. We could not leave one of our friends behind. We decided to divide the money that the seven of us had among the eight of us.

Eddie and a couple of others in our group were the most unfortunate; they had survived physically, but they were unable to cope as free men. They were like human jellyfish; spineless, afraid of everyone and everything, unable to make decisions or to defend themselves.

After receiving our provisions, we had to start getting ready for our journey to the west and southwest. But first we were to be taken by truck to the nearest main station on the Trans-Siberian railroad, namely Khabarovsk.

So now we were *grazhdanie,* (citizens) of the great Mother Russia, and we were being treated well, we thought. We soon found out that *politruk*'s predictions were 100 percent right.

We concluded that it wouldn't do any good to us or anybody to report to the camp authorities about the robbery. We also agreed that we just couldn't allow ourselves to leave Eddie behind for him to attempt to regain the lost money. We wanted to stay together, for the sake of safety and survival for all.

As for me, I seemed to have acquired a sudden spurt of energy, liveliness, even aggressiveness. My fluent command of the Russian language gave me self-confidence. Once we were set free on the Khabarovsk railway station with tickets, citizenship papers, and a money pouch, a new life and a tremendous reserve of new hope awakened in me and in most of us.

Physically, I had pains in my chest, spat blood with every cough, and was plagued with nasty, bleeding dysentery. I looked like a human shadow, a walking bag of bones with hardly any flesh. But I wanted very much to live, so I fought for my new life. As soon as I saw local women selling dairy products at the side of the railway station I asked, "Skolko? [how much?]" I didn't haggle over the price. I bought sweet cream, cheese, and butter, then I pulled out my large loaf of bread and I ate my fill.

At first I couldn't eat much in one sitting. My stomach had shriveled in size. I didn't eat more than my delicate system could properly absorb, but I ate more frequently. Food was not easily obtainable, but if one was alert, there were many choices; one had to wait for the right moment or go to the right place.

It was largely a matter of searching for a particular item; for a price it could be found. An uncontrollable greed could have fatal consequences. In several cases, former prisoners suffered serious digestive disorders, including twisted intestines, as the result of eating too much, too soon after being starved for months. I soon experienced a miraculous recovery. The more I ate, the more energy came to me, so I bought food at each stop the train made.

The *politruk* bought tickets for us to the city of Samarkand, but beyond purchasing the tickets, we had no guardian with us. We would have the freedom to take care of ourselves.

Oh, Blessed, Precious *Freedom*! Only those who have been deprived of it can fully appreciate its value. Now that our wings had been freed, we had to learn anew how to "fly" in this strange, frightening society.

We followed the same route by which we were brought east in cattle boxcars. But now we traveled in *miakhkiya* (first class) carriages, for there wasn't even standing room available in the *tviordiya* (coach) carriages. Heading back west, at least some of the station names were familiar to us. The cities of Chita, Ulan Ude, and the large lake port city of Irkutsk on Lake Baikal took on a more real meaning to us, since we were able to jump off the train, stretch our legs a little, and deal with the local people. A few other station names stand out in my memory—Petrovsk, Zima, Krasnoyarsk, and Tomsk—mainly because the local merchants had a particularly memorable assortment of goods that we were able to purchase. We were determined to stick together, the eight of us, since it was beneficial for all. When two or three of us were out hunting for food, the others guarded our space on the train, as well as the cache of food we had accumulated. Our solidarity particularly helped those two or three of our comrades who did not have the strength or mental alertness to reach our destination on their own.

In addition to the many thousands of prisoners returning west and south, many Soviet soldiers were traveling west toward the war zones in Europe. The third largest group of westward travelers was the families of Soviet citizens, particularly military personnel from the far eastern coast, most of them from Vladivostock, the major eastern Soviet port.

The reason for this mass movement of people westward was that the Japanese had, by then, occupied all of Manchuria. The Trans-Siberian Railroad was the only line of mass transportation available from the Far East to central Russia through most of the year. It ran for hundreds of miles at a very short distance from the Manchurian border. There was a fear, which soon developed into mass panic, that all of the far eastern territory might be cut off from the USSR and fall victim to the Japanese. As a part of the Axis powers, the Japanese were feared for their merciless cruelty to prisoners of war and to civilian populations. The Russians had never forgiven the Japanese for their defeat and loss of certain possessions in the far eastern territories in the war of 1905. Now the Russians resented the outcome of that war and feared that the Japanese would again attack the Soviet territories.

The trains were overcrowded far beyond their capacity with thousands of hungry, penniless people. There were frequent thefts, robberies, and muggings. If we hadn't banded together to protect what we had, especially the food, we would have easily lost everything. We were ragged, dirty, and emaciated; easy prey for quick and ruthless hoodlums. We looked scared, just like the miserable, recently released prisoners we were. Some of our boys still didn't speak much Russian. I felt more and more uncomfortable in my torn, dirty, smelly prison clothes.

One day while the train was standing in the station in the city of Irkutsk, a well-dressed, prosperous-looking Russian lady approximately in her mid-thirties was passing by and saw us sitting in the corner of the carriage with various "health" foods. We had our sacks open and were eating white cream cheese, thick farmer's cream, and dark rye bread with onions and herring.

She stopped and asked me, "Mozhetie, pozhaluysta, prodat' mnie odnoo selyot'ku? [Could you please sell me one herring?]"

I thought for a minute, then I spoke to her, "U menia deneg dovolno . . . [I have enough money for my needs now, but I would gladly exchange a herring for an article of clothing, for instance, a shirt. I would not sell it for money.]"

The lady cheerfully replied, "U menia mnogo krasivyh rubashok [I have many beautiful shirts]." She went back to the neighboring carriage and returned shortly, pulling out of her bag a beautiful, black, Cossack-style shirt with a high collar, embroidered with pretty, cheerful patterns. I offered her a nice, big herring for it. She didn't hesitate, but took it gladly and the deal was sealed. She went away satisfied.

I looked proudly at my new acquisition, especially its pretty patterns and the rich-looking, thick, silky material. It was excellently cut and made with long sleeves, with matching patterns embroidered on the cuffs. At first I hesitated before putting it on, as if I were afraid of losing it. I was simply fascinated with its rich, fine appearance. When I put that shirt on, I immediately felt much warmer, even without other heavy clothing. I must have looked proud and I felt as if I had grown a couple of inches.

I still had my goatskin fur jacket for warmth when I went out on my food-hunting expeditions. Even then I made sure that my new shirt showed through the open jacket. People noticed it, and it seemed to me that they gave me much better treatment than they might have given to a poor, raggedy urchin in prisoner's garb. They saw me as a young Cossack. The shirt helped me feel more like a normal person.

Each day I felt much stronger, and my morale was on the rise. We passed through many cities with strange Asiatic names. A few days after Irkutsk we came to the station of Novosibirsk. this was a key station for us, for here we turned south, toward the ancient cities of Tashkent and Samarkand.

Since we were headed for a warmer climate, I thought it a good time to part with my well-used goatskin fur jacket. I hesitated somewhat because I had grown up into it, and become sentimentally attached to it, but I offered it for sale at the railway station.

I stood in the station's busy terminal and draped my

fur on one shoulder, to make it obvious that I was trying to sell it. A young middle-aged Russian was passing by and became interested in it right away. He asked me, "Prodayotie? [Are you selling it?]"

"Dah [yes]," I said.

He made an offer of fifty rubles for it. I pretended to be making some calculations and asked if he would still be interested at a price of sixty rubles, to which he said, "Dah, voz'muh [yes, I'll take it]." The deal was finalized and we shook hands, according to the custom. As I parted with the jacket I felt as though I was betraying my uncle's goodwill, but reason prevailed and I took the man's money.

The station of Novosibirsk teemed with people of many races, dressed in a great variety of clothing. We had a difficult time staying together, and had to be careful to tightly hold onto our sacks of food and whatever personal mementos we still had. We looked out of the station at the streets, which looked very modern and clean, in spite of the great numbers of people walking to and fro or standing about. We didn't particularly want to tour the city, because we wanted to get as far away from the cold north as quickly as we could. We soon found out that the next train heading south, for Tashkent, was to leave that night. We decided to take this train because we knew that the train schedules were totally unreliable. Our next destination was about six days away.

The train headed due south. I still had some of my original food supplies from the Osnovnoya camp. My choice of onions proved to be wise. Both the onions and the herrings were still good and fresh. Onions, many Russians told me, were as good as *salo* (bacon). Indeed, in terms of nutrition, the onions were more useful than bacon, especially since there was an acute shortage of vegetables and fruits. No one minded the strong odor onions imparted, because it was considered a sign of good health. I began to feel less bothered by scurvy and my stomach felt much healthier. I had drunk many quarts of thick, nourishing cream and had eaten many kilos of cheese, and I continued to nibble away at hard, black bread spread with butter. In those circumstances, it was considered a meal fit for a king. I was well on the way to recovery from the many effects of hunger and the dysentery-infested prison camps.

Our journey to Tashkent was pleasant, since we were going south, leaving the inhospitable, cold northern country. The local climate improved greatly and the vegetation grew noticeably richer and more varied with each passing day. The valley of the Irtish River, the great granary of the area, was unbelievably rich in orchards and fertile fields. For us, after our experiences in the subarctic regions, it felt like the doors to paradise were gradually opening.

The train stopped in the thriving city of Semipalatinsk. We couldn't believe our eyes. We were able to buy apples, oranges, and several other fruits that I've never been able to identify. There was a fascinating fragrance in the air. The city was vibrant with crowds of people, talking loudly in strange languages unknown to us. The air was warm and clear. There were many stands loaded with dozens of different kinds of fruit and vegetables. It all looked unbelievably wonderful—we stared and hungrily breathed the lovely fragrance of it all.

After about a half-day stop, to cool the engines and restock needed supplies, we boarded again and continued in a southwesterly direction, toward Tashskent.

It was in Semipalatinsk we experienced our first involuntary parting. One of the members of our *dohodiagi* group apparently got lost in the crowd and didn't make it back to the train before the train started blowing the whistles for departure. He may have been trying to buy some food and forgot about the time limit. We were sorry to lose him, but we could do nothing about it. We couldn't stay in Semipalatinsk to look for him, because our tickets were only valid for a certain time period and the destination was specified. We never found out what happened to him.

The train made a stop at Alma-Ata, another beautiful, exotic city filled with and surrounded by fruit and vegetable orchards and luxurious vegetation.

We arrived in Tashkent in the wee hours of the morning, after riding all night in a tightly packed train. During the last several stops the train made before reaching the ancient city, we could not buy much food, except for some fruits and vegetables. Upon arriving in Tashkent we breathed a sigh of relief. The subarctic freeze was behind us hopefully forever. But the problems of living as free men in Soviet Russia were just beginning to present themselves. They came in quick succession, one upon the heels of the other.

Our first real encounter with the problems of coping with life as free men occurred shortly after arriving at the Tashkent railway station. In this nation, which had been totally controlled by the state police until the German invasion, people were used to being afraid of one another. The German invasion did not improve the fate of the common Russian people, because it brought new cruel suppression and mass killings. Before the war, everyone was aware of the fine, detailed network of spies where people constantly watched each other and kept the state police informed of everyone's private activities and even private whispers.

Now we were still confused and afraid of the crowds

milling around in each of the railway stations we stopped at on our trip south. Our stopovers were only several hours at the longest. Usually we dared not go far from the station. For one thing, we never knew if the train was going to stay at the station for five minutes or five hours. At Tashkent, however, we disembarked and planned to stay long enough to get up-to-date information on the status of the Polish military units that we were told would be formed there.

Gienek Kowalczyk, a member of our group, discovered just as we got off the train that his documents were missing. He didn't know exactly when he had them last or where they disappeared. The fact was before us: he had no identification. We all agreed that he should go to the local Polish agency that had been established in Tashkent for stranded Polish refugees with problems such as his. One who traveled without documents was certainly exposing himself to the chance of being sent back to the rehabilitation camps. NKVD squads were constantly on the lookout, making sweeps of the streets, and the undocumented unfortunates were being shipped away to unknown destinations.

We were among thousands upon thousands of former prisoners of various races, origins, colors, and shapes—among them Poles, Ukrainians, and Jews—who were looking for a place to lie down under the blue skies. In addition, thousands of Russians, Russian Ukrainians, and Bielorussians, who were displaced by the invading German armies, had traveled east and south to escape the war zones.

The daily news from the German-occupied territories brought grim eyewitness reports of German atrocities and the merciless total destruction of the inhabitants in most of the villages and towns that the Germans had conquered.

The Russian armies, with their obsolete and ill-maintained equipment, were no match against the German storm troops. The thousand-year-old German dream of *Drang nach Osten* (a push to the East) was being realized with a deep-seated hatred and vengeance. They moved eastward without much effective resistance by the Soviet armies. Those who weren't quick enough to escape the German onslaught were killed ruthlessly, so that following troops would have no problems and no threats from the enemy population.

The Ukrainian leaders in Russia who had made political deals with Hitler (he had promised them a free and independent Ukrainian state) were finding out that Hitler had no use for an independent Ukraine. Now that the victorious panzer divisions were cutting into the Ukraine and Russia proper, all the way to the gates of Moscow itself, Hitler could afford to disregard and forget promises made earlier.

Thus, Tashkent received thousands of desperate, hungry, tattered people, singly and in family groups, who had just managed to escape with their lives, but nothing else. The local NKVD commands were doing their best to keep people on the trains, so that they would go farther east, to have them farther away from the invading Germans. By the time we arrived in Tashkent, the hungry masses of war refugees were filling up all available space under the hot, cloudless, open skies. We were lucky to have been allowed to get off the train at the Tashkent station.

We stood in a row on the sidewalk in front of the station, the six of us that remained of the original group of eight from Osnovnaya camp. I stood at one end of the row. Each of us had a little linen sack containing our survival rations. Various people passed in front of us from both directions, but for the most part we ignored them.

At one point three young Russian thugs, about seventeen to nineteen years old, passed by, and one of them, without stopping, bent down slightly, picked up one of our sacks, and kept walking on. We were all looking in different directions, none of us watching our supplies. In a flash I sensed that something was wrong, that one food sack was missing. As the thief passed in front of me, something snapped inside me. Without warning, I let my foot fly swiftly, right into the thief's groin. Evidently it was well aimed, for the culprit gave out a sharp groan, doubled over, dropped the sack, and ran. That incident reminded us to be more alert and observant. We held on to our possessions, and always assigned someone to stand guard over our things if one or two of us had to be somewhere else.

Officially, the city of Tashkent, the capital of the Uzbek Soviet Republic, was out of bounds for Russian war refugees and released Polish prisoners, as well as those who had been forcefully resettled from Poland. In spite of these rules and the sweeps of the illegal residents in the city, made by the NKVD secret police—people were picked up from the streets by the hundreds—there were still hundreds of thousands of homeless drifters around the city. They came into the city in droves and stayed there, hiding every so often, whenever the rumors warned of the impending threats of NKVD raids. With all the dangers of abuse by the NKVD police, and by the thousands of hungry pickpockets and habitual robbers, there were still many places where at least those with legitimate IDs (e.g., passports or prison-camp release documents) could get some food and shelter, and perhaps medical or first-aid care. They could also find clean drinking water in those posts. Those, however, who could not show any personal documents, were in many cases swept off the streets and ended up in some remote labor camp.

Nonetheless, there must still have been a few hundred thousand in Tashkent, there being nowhere else to go, but to the big cities. At least Tashkent had organized food and water distribution systems, and a semblance of administrative and social services.

There were no accommodations available for us in Tashkent. Luckily the weather was balmy; it was neither too cold nor too hot. The next two nights we slept in the streets, huddled close together, with our precious sacks under our heads. Food was scarce. In the morning we saw people sitting on the sidewalks, begging for food with outstretched arms. By noon these same beggars were lying down, lifeless, next to the buildings. A farmer's horse-drawn cart drove through the city as two assistants loaded the dead bodies onto the cart to be buried in a mass grave on the outskirts of the city; a very gruesome sight it was.

Tashkent was an ancient city, with a history of some three thousand years. It had thrived in past centuries, being situated on the trade routes of the Mongolian nomadic tribes who traveled in pursuit of trade connections with other Asiatic and European peoples. The city showed its proud, prosperous past in its minarets and mosques, whose portals and front walls were encrusted with richly multicolored, centuries-old ceramic mosaic. The mosaic was in a state of neglect; in some parts, fragments had fallen off or were chipped off by wandering maruaders or hoodlums. However, the splendor of the outlines of the ancient khans, and of the great chiefs on horseback, with wide, heavy swords, made me recall the fascinating stories told to us by one of the lecturers in prison cell 203 about the travels and exploits of Genghis Khan throughout these territories. Such thoughts flashed through my mind sometimes, as I came upon an extraordinary building, a statue, or a picture set in the mosaic exterior of an ancient structure. I connected them with some stories I had heard before in the prison lectures. And here I was, actually looking at these ancient wonders.

The situation for us in Tashkent was unpromising. There were a great many thousands of Polish men and women who came here from the prison camps when the amnesty was effected. We heard accounts from many of them; some had gone through worse hell than we had. Occasional stray shootings by the hateful brigadiers (for not working fast enough or not fulfilling the quota), starvation, and beatings had left the majority of people dead and buried in snow graves. The haggard, hungry, ghost-like appearance of those who made it to the south testified amply that they were telling the truth. We believed it, because we knew what it was like. Here in Tashkent we came across a different kind of misery.

The warm, sunny south, with pleasant temperatures and plentiful vegetation, proved to be a deathtrap for hundreds of thousands of former Polish prisoners and resettlers. Millions of prisoners, enslaved by the mammoth Soviet slave-labor camp network in the northern country, had dreamed of how lovely it would be in the warm climate. Many unpleasant surprises awaited those who finally reached Kazachstan and Uzbekistan. In a way, the subzero temperatures of cold northern climate was more conducive to physical survival because germs and bacteria had much less of a chance to incubate and develop.

In the south, the emaciated and still hungry masses of the Polish aimless and homeless men, women, and children were decimated by typhoid fever, dysentery, scurvy, and other local diseases. The warm humidity of the south was a perfect breeding ground for many kinds of bacteria and viruses, and the poorly fed and improperly housed Polish refugees succumbed by the thousands.

Along with the thousands of Polish men, who came to the Uzbekstan Soviet Republic from the prisons and prison camps scattered across the European and Asiatic USSR, came civilians who had been taken from their homes in Poland. They came by train, by riverboat on the Syr Darya and Amu Darya, or by whatever other means of transportation they managed to find. They were mostly older people and women with young children. The men in the eligible military age bracket had been either interned as soldiers or shipped away to the rehabilitational labor camps. When wives found out that the Polish military units would be formed in the south, they packed up their families as best they could and headed south to the big cities of Buchara, Tashkent, and Samarkand in Uzbekstan.

The immediate situation was indeed desperately difficult and hopeless. We contacted a Polish refugee information center, trying to find out where and when we could enlist into the Polish Army. The reply was that it would not be soon; weeks or even months might pass before any recruitment offices were set up. We were told that we would be much safer and better off in a smaller city like Samarkand, which was about ninety miles southeast of Tashkent.

"The sooner you get away from this capital city, the better off you'll be," said the Polish Army major in charge of the information center. "You will find more help and more information in Samarkand."

The remaining six of us set off for Samarkand. We preferred to stay together for safety. By now we had grown very close and we had learned to depend on each other in times of need, whatever the need might be.

11
Shalom-Aleikom (Peace Be with You)

The train ride to Samarkand didn't take more than three or four hours. In Samarkand we met, to our dismay, as much of an overcrowded situation as we had left behind us in Tashkent.

In Samarkand the density of people was much greater per square mile than in Tashkent. Crowds of miserable, walking skeletons, helpless and devoid of human spirit were in the railway station. The most prominent features on their faces were their eyes, which looked too large for their shriveled faces; eyes which begged for mercy, food, and, in many cases, death. One could see that the flame of life flickered very faintly in their faces.

Here, for the first time, we noticed small children, four to ten years old, whose bodies had never had a chance to take a good hold on life. They huddled next to their mothers or grandmothers or unrelated "aunts" and "cousins" who had appointed themselves these children's guardians. They wore hopeless, hungry faces, faces that had never quite learned how to smile. They no longer begged for food. They knew that the people they met would have no food to give them. The elders caring for these children, many of whom were orphans, could no longer encourage them to smile, for they themselves had little hope left in their hearts.

Walking through the crowded streets, we finally found the Polish refugee information center. An office was set up, but it had no facilities or provisions, even though large numbers of people came begging for food every day. These people were a mixed lot of miseries. They were scared and anxious for their starving children, many of whom had been born shortly before they were driven out of their warm homes into the darkness of night without court trial or verdict, or even a chance to ask why or where they were being taken. The fathers objected, protested, argued, and begged, but the strange, cruel men beat them down to the ground with rifle butts and then told them to stand on the side. The fathers were then put in police vans and driven off, never to be seen again. The mothers were told to pack their belongings, whatever they could carry with them, and the next day the mothers and children were taken to a cold train for a long journey. The children were hungry and cold. Wives and children wanted so much to see their loved ones again, but they were taken to unknown destinations without any means of communications. When their train journey ended at last, after several weeks, they were let out into a snowbound taiga forest and told that it was their new home. Log barracks were provided for them, but no food. The adults had to work first, before they could get food for their families. The settlements were organized so that a few women were assigned to care for the small children of several families.

When the Germans attacked Russia in July 1941, Stalin realized right away that Russia alone was not prepared to defend itself. The USSR convoy contacted the heads of the Polish government, in exile in London, about making a deal for freeing the Polish prisoners from their captivity and using them in the war against the Germans. This political transaction was termed an *amnesty*, a very unfortunate and unfair term in this case. The term *amnesty* implies that a guilt existed, or a crime had been committed, and the person who committed an unlawful act is now being pardoned. But there was no wrongful act committed by these 2 million people—men, women, and their innocent children. There was, however, a damning guilt and crime among these people in the government that now was proclaiming the amnesty. Breaking of the basic human law had been committed on the other side—by the aggressors. The deceitful term *amnesty* was devised by Stalin's cunning advisers mainly to disguise their guilt, to divert the attention of the Western powers away from the Soviet guilt, and also to put a smokescreen over the crime they were perpetrating at the time.

Men and women able to serve in the military service would be needed and would know what the future would offer them.

What about the fate of older people, those sick and unfit for the military? And what about the hundreds of thousands of innocent and helpless children? Would they ever have their rights restored to be back in their fatherland, in their families' homes? Thousands upon thousands of these stolen children had been taken away from their rightful parents and put into communist children's homes and conscripted into Comsomol (Communist Youth) brigades.

When the announcement of the amnesty finally reached the people in the settlements, their joy had no bounds. At the first opportunity they headed south to the Uzbek Soviet Republic, where it was said that the Polish Army was to be organized. A few families were reunited, but most were fatherless, since their men had been destroyed by the cruelty of their captors. Families continued to search, but their hopes were usually in vain.

For several days we tried to get clear information on the status of the formation the Polish Army, but no one could tell us anything definite. It was the beginning of February 1942. The nights were cold, and the only sleeping accommodations we could find were spaces in the open fields around the city of Samarkand. On our repeated visits to the Polish refugee information center we learned that the local Soviet authorities were stalling by delaying the assignment of any facilities and equipment, and the recruitment of staff. About the middle of February, Captain Urbanski, the officer running the temporary center, told us openly that he didn't expect any enlisting to be done for at least five to six weeks. He advised us quite earnestly to go outside the city, to one of the surrounding Uzbek villages, and bide our time there until definite news came regarding the army recruitment.

"If you stick around here," Captain Urbanski told us, "you will have to sleep out in the open, without regular meals or help. We have too many hungry, sick, and desperate people to take care of. You had better go to one of the villages; the Uzbeks will give you food. Just walk in a southerly direction until you come to a village."

While we talked to Captain Urbanski, a woman about twenty-seven years old listened to our conversation. Later, when we were discussing his proposition and formulating a plan of action, Janina Kotyrba spoke up.

"If you guys are seriously thinking about getting out of the city, perhaps you'll not mind if I go with you. I could help you out with chores, cook for you. I'll try not to be a burden."

We looked at her more seriously now. So far we had managed by ourselves pretty well, we thought. I was the youngest of our group, almost eighteen years of age. Anthony Pasierba was twenty-five; Kazik Rzutny, 23; Mietek Lizak, 26; Stanley Tkacz, 30; and Robert Malinowski, about 25. So far in our travels together we had never talked, or even thought much of women. It was, indeed, like the commissar Kapusta at the Lutsk prison had predicted: we had managed to survive, but none of us felt any sexual desire. We had a brief discussion among ourselves and decided we would take Janina with us. She appeared relatively healthy and resourceful, if somewhat emaciated and hungry.

Early the next morning we started out. We each had our little sack with bits of spare food, for a leaner hour. We crossed a wide plain, with no hills and not many trees. There were grazing fields for sheep and, in other places, large rice fields. The latter required a lot of irrigation, so the Uzbeks had engineered an elaborate system of canals and reservoirs to distribute the water. The land was level, so the water flow had to be artificially directed by means of a clever system consisting of a waterwheel driven mainly by man power.

We kept walking south on a dirt road. The few natives we met along the road were reserved at first and unwilling to talk to us, until we told them we were not Russians, but former Polish prisoners. Then they really opened up to us. We briefly told them our story—in particular, about our relationship to the Russians in our own country and how they drove us away from our homes, into slavery in Siberia. The Uzbeks sympathized with us completely, because they had been subjugated and enslaved by the same power. They spoke the Russian language rather unwillingly, however, and soon they were teaching us their Uzbek tongue.

We had walked about fifteen miles out of Samarkand

when one of our Uzbek friends suggested that we stay for a while at his cousin's farm.

"My cousin Ahmed Bashir is well-to-do. He will welcome you all, give you food and shelter, and treat you well. You could help him, perhaps, with some field work."

"Thank you, kind sir," we said. "May Allah be praised and may he reward you generously for your kindness."

We had been taught some of their social customs and were feeling more and more at ease with them. Our friend's name was Mahomet Kaisovi. He was walking home after having transacted some business in a nearby village. His home was farther on, past Ahmed Bashir's farm entrance. He went into Mr. Bashir's home with us and explained our plight to the latter, saying that we needed food and temporary shelter. Mahomet further said that we were willing to work at whatever Mr. Bashir would need done on the farm or around his animal shed or houses. We bowed gratefully and shook Mahomet's hand before he went on his way home.

Mr. Bashir was a kind man, about fifty years old, with a generous gray beard. His eyes shone with a sparkle that reflected the internal happiness and contentment of the man. He called an assistant, or perhaps it was the foreman of the farm, and they talked between themselves in the Uzbek language.

Then Mr. Bashir turned to us and said in Russian, "Go with Mr. Koulab. He will set you up for the night. You need to rest well for a few days. After that we will find things for you to do."

We followed Mr. Koulab to a large building, which appeared to be a barn. At the far end there were some chicken coops. By the main entrance, there was a large area filled with sacks of rice, perhaps waiting for shipment. In this area there was also a pile of rice straw, and Mr.

Koulab indicated that we could sleep there. There was a small shed in the corner, which was assigned to Janina, or Jasia, as we called her. She rarely participated in our general conversations or planning, and just tagged along.

During the next few days we had a chance to rest and eat and cook for ourselves. Mr. Koulab gave us a sack of rice, salt, and some vegetables, and we were allowed to pick more vegetables from the fields. These made rather tasty and nourishing meals. Many root vegetables, such as potatoes, carrots, and some local varieties whose names we didn't know, had not been thoroughly picked from the fields during the harvest, so we could easily find more edible plants there. In addition, Mr. Koulab continued to be generous. Every so often he gave us some mutton or a couple of chickens. The cooking was done outdoors over a fire built between several stones. It was slow, but we had plenty of time. It was quite enjoyable to have, at last, plenty of good, warm, fresh air and a sufficient amount of food. This slow and easy style of life gave us an excellent opportunity to rebuild our physical health. Also, these living conditions, with strangers who turned out to be our benefactors, proved to be ideal for us to strengthen our self-image and our faith in humanity.

At last we had plenty of food, enough free time to cook it, and a fine climate. We could only dream about all these luxuries until recently. We were treated with kindness and generosity by all the Uzbeks, when they found out that we, like themselves, were people who had been ruthlessly suppressed, subjugated, and forcefully driven out of our homes. The Uzbeks were interested in us as people, and even invited us to their homes. We did some work for them, cleaning yards and fields, and fixing buildings that were in need of repair.

Mr. Bashir wanted his estate made festive because he

had a big event coming up—one of his two beautiful daughters was getting married. She was nineteen years old and a real beauty. To our great surprise, our host invited us, the homeless wandering beggars, to the wedding ceremony and feast. He didn't want to leave anyone out of this joyous occasion. At dawn on the day of the wedding a ram was slaughtered, skinned and prepared for roasting. It was hung over a fire pit, allowing enough cooking time to be ready for the afternoon feast. In the big, ranch-style house there was plenty of food and wine waiting for the guests.

The host was happy and jubilant, shaking hands with and hugging all who came. That was the first time that I saw the inside of the main house. There were kerosene torches burning in all four corners of the large ceremonial hall, providing light and enhancing the festive atmosphere. I was surprised to see no table or chairs. There was a smooth dirt floor with a ditch neatly dug out in the shape of a horseshoe. The ditch was for the legs and feet, so that one could sit down on the floor and eat comfortably.

The ram had finished roasting by mid-afternoon. Huge cuts of it were brought into the dining hall on large brass trays, and the feast began. Large urns filled with homemade red wine stood at either end of the dining area, wherein each guest could dip a brass mug and drink to his or her heart's content. In the middle of the horseshoe a giant brass bowl was placed, brimming with curried rice mixed with small chunks of mutton.

It was a feast for all the senses. The enticing smell of the exotically seasoned mutton, the mountainous heap of curried rice, the chalices of ruby-red wine—it all titillated our palates. About thirty people were seated around the festive "table." Everyone had easy access to the bowl of rice, which was served and eaten with bare hands. The mutton and the rice were delicious, not only because we had been starved for so long, but because it was expertly cooked in the traditional Uzbek style.

Now the bride and groom entered. The bride's petite figure was gowned in exquisitely embroidered Oriental silks of many colors. Her face was veiled up to her eyes, which sparkled with happiness. The groom came from the opposite side of the room, in formal attire, topped by a turban on his head. Apparently they had not met before the wedding day—it was a prearranged marriage—but they looked totally pleased with each other and very happy.

The climax to the ceremony was the entertainment provided after everyone had their first helping of the feast, shortly after the young nuptial couple sat down. After long and hearty applause for the young couple and when everyone had satisfied his or her appetite with the delicious mutton and curried rice, the master of ceremonies announced that next there would be the artistic part of the ceremony. This was the peak of the day's festivities. Three beautiful girls came out to the center of the horseshoe to present the exquisite, fascinating art of Oriental belly dancing. The dancers were thoroughly enjoying themselves, exhibiting mastery and skill in moving and gyrating their bodies. It seemed as though each limb and muscle of their delicately shaped bodies vibrated and responded on its own to the music played by the flute and tambourine. It was evident that the dancers were pleased with themselves. They were carrying out all their movements with total ecstasy and abandonment, with an inner peace, graceful poise, and beautiful maidenly smiles. The day's activities and the celebration of the feast were enjoyable and unforgettable. It seemed unreal—like a film—it was so far removed from our recent life experiences. It was difficult to believe in the authenticity of this beautiful and colorful event, after which we had to face a very unpleasant surprise.

Our fellow traveler, Jasia, didn't feel well on the day of the wedding ceremony and stayed in our quarters. We didn't suspect even for a moment that her life was coming to an end. The next day she felt much weaker, and on the second day she died in her room in the shed. She was a good person who had suffered and survived through an incredible amount of suffering. It was a tragedy that she died just at a time when it seemed that before long she could finally begin to enjoy a happy adult life. However, we had trained ourselves to accept the will of the Creator. Death was now an inseparable part of our lives.

There was no Catholic priest nearby to administer the final rites or to assist in the prayers for her soul, so we just gathered at her burial and each said a silent prayer that her afterlife would be more peaceful than her life on Earth was. Her death shook us up and brought us back to reality after that delightful wedding day. But there were no tears at Jasia's funeral. It was quiet and peaceful—we couldn't cry anymore. With the silent prayers came a deeply felt anger of frustration and helplessness. We could hardly turn our thoughts to God for succor, because it seemed to us that He had turned His attention away from us for too long a time. Where was He in the presence of all this suffering? We had been taught to have infinite trust in His judgment, to be patient forever, if necessary. But this kind of blind, unquestioning trust and faith had begun to die in us. We wanted a fairer chance to defend ourselves against evil. When time came for us to move, a new blood of hope entered into our veins.

Soon came the time for us to move, again into the unknown. News reached us on the farm from Samarkand that the recruiting office had been set up and that we would soon be able to enlist in the Polish Army.

Sometime during the last two days of our stay at Mr. Bashir's, Kazik Rzutny and I went out for a walk in the fields. We just wanted to fill ourselves with the beauty of the surrounding country. The weather was fabulously serene and clear; the sun was out, but it was not too hot. The clouds high above glided by, gently tugging their shadows across the rice paddies. After we had walked about a mile into the fields, we saw a man walking along the opposite side of the rice paddy. He was a middle-aged man, wearing a wide Chinese hat.

He surprised us by shouting an Uzbek greeting, "Shalom-Aleikom," which we learned to mean "Peace be with you."

We both answered with a loud, "Aleikom-Shalom [and with you, too]," and he went happily on, drinking wine out of a gallon-size earthenware jug.

He rested the jug on his right elbow, tipping it into his mouth. He was humming quietly a soulful Uzbek song. He seemed to be entirely at peace with himself and in total harmony with all the beauty and wisdom of the nature surrounding us. The sight of him brought us peace and restored more of our faith in God's everlasting healing power. He left us with a long-lasting image of a carefree, happy man.

We had rested physically and our spiritual strength had returned enough to start thinking about returning to Samarkand. We told Mr. Bashir of our plans and thanked him for his kind hospitality and generosity. When we told him that we were hoping to get a chance to leave the Soviet Union, he said that he had no use or sympathy for the Russians.

"I wish they would leave us Uzbeks alone to govern

ourselves," he said. "We want to attend our mosque. We want to raise our children in our traditional ways. We want to carry on our trade without their restrictions, and we don't want them to take our sheep away from us." Mr. Bashir went on and on, his anger intensifying as he spoke.

When it came time for us to leave, Mr. Bashir insisted that we fill up our food sacks for leaner days. We carried away not only food, which was crucially important for our survival in Samarkand, but also resurrected faith in human kindness and rekindled hope for our survival. He and his household residents had shown us that people could still act humanely to one another. They restored in us a basic belief in the kindness of the human spirit. Thus fortified, physically and spiritually, we left Mr. Bashir's home and farm, leaving Jasia behind. May her next life be kinder to her.

In the Polish Army

12

The conditions in Samarkand had not changed much when we returned there. Just as many people were out in the streets as there had been when we left. People were dying in the streets from hunger and exhaustion. But this time the recruiting office was open. Our second day in the city we went to be examined by the recruiting doctor and the military commission. All six of us were in good enough physical condition to enlist in the Seventh Infantry Division. Actually, given the circumstances, we didn't have to be bursting with exceptionally good health to be considered favorably for military service.

The main goal of the Polish government, in exile in London, was to somehow get as many Polish people out of Russia as possible. As long as the Soviets were hard-pressed by the advancing Nazi armies, they were amenable to any negotiations. The Soviets had interned almost 2 million Polish people in prisons and in slave-labor camps, including the treacherously imprisoned scores of Polish military units, and they were determined to keep them there. When the Soviets found themselves under the brutal pressure of the Nazi blitzkrieg, Josef Stalin showed a great deal of calculating political pragmatism in allowing the Polish leaders to take several hundred thousand Polish subjects, incarcerated in the USSR slave system, out of Russia.

Tens of thousands of Polish soldiers were captured by

the Soviets in the eastern part of Poland under the guise of a friendly gesture of protecting them from the German onslaught. They were subsequently shipped to the hard-labor camps, where most of them perished from being worked under inhuman conditions in subzero temperatures and gross undernourishment.

Approximately 230,000 Polish soldiers were captured by the Red Army in 1939 and 1940. Officers were interned mainly in POW camps; enlisted men, in general, were sent to labor camps in hundreds of locations, some near the Pechora River in Northeast European Russia; the rest were scattered all around the vast Siberia, including the territories of Kamchatka Peninsula and the Kolyma River. Of these 230,000 soldiers taken by the Russians, only approximately 82,000 surivived. About seventy-five thousand joined General Anders's army in 1942 and were evacuated from Russia the same year. Another seven thousand joined the Kosciuszko Division and stayed in Russia, fighting under their command. The rest perished, were murdered in officers' camps, or died as a result of hard labor, inadequate food, and harsh treatment.

About fifteen thousand Polish officers were summarily shot to death in special camps, e.g., Katyn, in May 1940, and in several other locations. These were officers who were confined in three POW camps: Starobielsk (125 miles east of Kharkov), Kozielsk (95 miles south of Smolensk), and Ostashkov (halfway between Moscow and Leningrad). They were buried in mass graves, which even now, in the 1980s, are being discovered. The Soviet government was determined to destroy all intelligentsia, the thousands of men and women who belonged to the leading and governing class of the nation. Such people were immediately sought out and incarcerated and mostly liquidated as soon as the Soviets first entered Poland's territory. Even with such an agreement, local Soviet authorities put many obstacles in the way of the efforts of the Polish leaders, so as to reduce to a minimum the number of Polish subjects let out of the USSR. The NKVD refused travel permits for civilians in the resettlement camps who were anxious to get to the areas where there were army recruiting centers. Nor did they allow loyal Polish minorities—Jews, Ukrainians, and others locked up in prisons and prison camps—to join the Polish Army. They made it virtually impossible to locate and collect the Polish children left parentless in different parts of Russia. There were thousands of orphaned Polish children whose parents were forcefully separated from them or had died from starvation or epidemics. The Polish leaders had succeeded in gathering about five hundred of these unfortunate innocents and shipped one big transport of them to India. The Indian government had agreed to accept under their care as many orphaned Polish children as would be freed by the Russians. Many thousands of children were forcefully separated from their parents and sent into the communist children's homes, never to be heard of again.

After being inducted into the army we had a few days without any definite duties. We waited for our military uniforms to be delivered. There were problems in getting uniforms and other military paraphernalia from our host government, even though they were not actually supplying them. The uniforms, equipment, and supplies were all furnished by the western Allies.

However, we didn't have much to worry about. We were fed two meals a day and given the luxury of sleeping under a roof, on a straw-stream, dry mud floor, rather than in nature's bosom, with just a brick for a pillow. We had to sleep out in the open field for about three weeks while we waited for the recruitment office to enlist us. During the day we had a lot of spare time. We went for walks around the city to see the sights and, perhaps, occasionally bump into an old acquaintance.

One sunny day we were walking along the streets through the large crowds. Here and there dead bodies were being picked up and loaded onto horsedrawn carts to be delivered to the common burial graves. At one point we noticed a crowd of people gathered in a large, open space near a mosque. They were standing in a circle, anxiously watching some action in the center. My friend Kazik Rzutny and I, driven by curiosity, squeezed ourselves into the front ring of the circle. What we saw was like an arena—one huge, drunken Soviet sailor was beating up on a couple of tattered, exhausted Polish former prisoners. The sailor was a man in his mid-twenties, a big, husky man wearing a navy jacket and a cap with the inscription *Odessa* on a narrow band around the base of the cap. Apparently he was in the Soviet Black Sea Navy. The man looked more like a pirate from the illustrious sea stories I had devoured as a child. He had a long, bushy moustache, red face, drunken wild eyes, and an open mouth contorted with cynical laughter. His looks and behavior showed a man totally insensitive and callous to human pain, and capable of inflicting pain or killing a man without any hesitation. The two young men obviously were no match for the sailor; their combined strength was totally ineffective against him. They looked so emaciated that they could hardly stand up on their own legs. He literally threw one man at the other. He swayed and swerved and almost fell several times from his drunkenness.

The spectators standing in the wide circle shifted and backed away as the fighters within changed their places.

One or two men would shout to the sailor, in Russian, "Odoydi od neeh, tyh bolshoy obezyana [go away from them, you big ape]."

But that only aroused the sailor even more. As he looked in the direction from where the voice came, people standing there made ready to scuttle. Nobody really wanted to risk direct confrontation with the big brute.

I recognized one of the two men in the arena as Thad Lubek, the policeman's son who testified against me to the NKVD investigator during my interrogations in the Lutsk prison. He didn't quite look the same, but the more I looked at him in that arena, the more certain I was that it was Thadek L.

The sailor reminded me of the Philistine Goliath towering over David, who was armed with only a slingshot. It seemed like such an uneven match. The rest of us just stood around watching one of our kind being viciously abused. I looked at the mesmerized faces of the people standing there, but none was brave enough to do something. I felt the urge to act the part of David. I saw a large beer bottle on the ground near me. I picked it up, even though I didn't feel I'd have the guts to use it. But when the sailor was near me, swaying in his drunken chase after one of his victims, with his jeering eyes and frothing mouth, I couldn't stand it any more. I extended my arm holding the bottle and quickly smashed it on his head as hard as I could. I saw his eyes stare at me desperately for a moment, then he crashed to the ground. I slipped out among people's legs, and I ran as fast as my shaking legs could carry me, until I felt more or less safe in our military barracks. I undressed, got under the covers, and pretended I was sick.

That was not the last time I would see the big sailor. I later learned that as soon as the sailor collapsed to the ground the crowd quickly dispersed. He came to after a while and went to a clinic, where he got a few stitches and a large bandage, fashioned into a turban that almost covered his entire head.

The next two days I stayed inside our barracks, lying down on my place on the floor, playing sick. The sailor came by on the second day. He looked miserable, with bandages still covering most of his head. He must have been in a daze, because even though he turned his probing eyes in my direction, they didn't even hesitate on me. He passed me by. All the time my frightened heart raced at what felt like a thousand beats per minute. I lay still on the floor, looked sick, and prayed hard to God to divert the ugly brute away from me. When the sailor left our barrack I released the air that I had been holding in my lungs. I sighed with relief. I hoped to God that he would not return to take a second look at me, for the next time I might show my nervousness and betray myself.

The thought of Thad L. being in Samarkand aroused my curiosity. I saw him being beat up by the sailor, I was quite sure of that, but since I had to run I didn't know where I could find him again. I knew he had been shipped to a labor camp with a sentence of ten years, but I had no idea where he had ended up. I had forgotten the unpleasant experience I had with him at the time of the interrogations. I had forgiven him for testifying against me. He had been punished just as badly as we all had. I didn't know exactly which camp he was shipped to, but I knew he suffered enough. Only Zenon K. and I, from our group of ten who were sentenced together in Lutsk, were lucky enough to be able to share the hardships of the long journey and the labor camp, but we lost track of each other near the end of our stay in the camp because of several reshufflings of the prisoners while we were being processed for release. I hoped that Thad and I would soon meet again somewhere.

Our military barrack was soon filled up. Our commanders talked about moving us away somewhere, to make room for new recruits. In a few days we received orders to get ready to move the next morning. We were to march about twelve to fifteen miles to the small town of Kermine.

It was an overnight march, and the nights were quite cold. We were not given any supplies of food or water for the march, supposedly so as not to be overburdened. Since most of us had not recovered from being undernourished for many months, we were allowed to take a rest at the halfway point. The rest was ordered near a small pond, so all of us ran for water. The water proved to be infested and unfit for drinking, and we all ended up with pneumonia and bad cases of dysentery. That was the first time I really missed my uncle's goatsksin fur. I shivered through the night and the next morning, while burning with fever. The medics took a large number of us to the military hospital in Kermine. The doctor said I had pneumonia, a bad case of pneumonia.

13
The Song of the Cornucopia

This field military hospital in Kenimeh became a health service institution by accident. Nobody had planned for it to be a hospital. It was an old Uzbek warehouse, mostly abandoned in the recent times with three large rooms that from necessity, had become patient wards in which medical wonders were supposed to happen.

The conditions of our forced march between Kermine and Kenimeh largely caused my catching a bad cold, which soon developed into pneumonia.

After we arrived at this hospital, space was found for us all on the concrete floor with some rice straw strewn around. The sick lay on the floor, side by side, without any analysis of their illnesses before admitting them into the hospital. Apparently they were being brought in at such a high rate that there was not sufficient time or trained personnel to classify and segregate various cases of contagious diseases.

Thus people with dysentery, malaria, typhoid fever, pneumonia, and some more unusual diseases that the doctors could not identify were placed indiscriminately next to someone who may have been going through the advanced stages of another killer disease. The most prevalent, and most dreaded disease, was the typhoid fever, whose harvest of death was always the heaviest.

Pneumonia, which had brought me into the hospital, had grown into a double pneumonia. My weak body was not able to ward off an attack of the typhoid fever, so in addition to pneumonia, scurvy, and bleeding dysentery, I succumbed to typhoid. I don't know all that transpired during my battle for survival at that time, but I know that the temperature of my body shot up past the limits of normal tolerance and I lay there in a semi-conscious state for several days.

Many newly dead bodies were taken out of the hospital daily, vacating the needed space on the cold cement floor for more victims to be brought in. This was going on around the clock.

My stay in this incubator of contagious diseases lasted about five days. When my high fever soon reached such intensity that I began to hallucinate, I found myself on the narrow edge separating life from death.

I feel I'm sinking deeper and deeper. It's so dark! Who are these little people with big, bulging eyes, trying to cheer me up? Where am I? These little people all speak Polish—I must be back in Poland. They extend their tiny fingers to touch me. They won't hurt me. They are my friends.

Now I am soaring high in the sky, at the head of a formation of cranes. The cranes surround me and lead me. I can no longer do what I want. They control my movements.

The doctor gives me a pill and tells me I have to take it.

"Why?" I ask. "Why, doctor?"

"You take it—it'll put you in a good mood. You may even fall asleep."

"But I don't really want to fall asleep. I'm too busy. What are you giving to me, doctor?"

"It's only aspirin, soldier, take it. I don't have anything else to give you now."

"Doctor, why is this man lying on my right so pale? Who's he, anyway? Kazik R. was here yesterday. Did he get well so fast? Dr. Bronikowski, what happened to Kazik, and what happened to the other men who were here? Why do they change these sick men so often? Where do they disappear to?"

"They are all in heaven now," says the doctor.

"I don't like it. I must speak to my sister Maria. Oh, there she is! I hear her calling me."

"Richard, where are you? When are you coming back home?" she asks.

I see her quite clearly, but I can barely hear her. The picture changes all the time. The panorama keeps rolling. Maria is in sight again. She beckons me to join her in singing. She is very happy, smiling. She starts singing "Halka," the unforgettable aria from Moniuszko's opera.

"Szumią jodły na gór szczycie,
    szumią sobie w dal. . . .
[The fir trees are rustling on the mountain peaks,
    rustling away. . . .]"

I love that song, so I join Maria, full voice, for a harmonious duet. Now a huge, multicolored cornucopia appears on the scene, behind Maria. All of its bounties come spilling out of it. Fruit, candies, cookies—all in such an appetizing pattern. Maria looks so lovely, so inviting, so happy.

We continue our duet:

". . . Mnie samemu smętne zycie, bo mam
    w sercu zal. . . .
[Sad is my life, for my heart's burdened
    with grief. . . .]"

> Maria stops singing. "Richie, I miss you. When are you coming back?"
> "I want to visit our mother, Maria. Will you wait for me?"
> "I will, but hurry up. I will not wait forever."
> Then Maria's face saddens and she starts singing another song:

> > "Jak szybko mijają chwile,
> > jak szybko mija czas.
> > Za rok, za dzień, za chwilę,
> > razem nie będzie nas,
> > I nasze mode lata upyną,
> > szybko w dal,
> > A w sercu pozostanie tęsknota,
> > smutek, żal.

> > [How quickly pass the minutes,
> > how quickly flies the time,
> > In a year, a day, a moment,
> > we shall part forever,
> > And the years of our youth
> > will fast flow away.
> > In our hearts we'll carry
> > nostalgia, sadness, and lament.]

> We sing happily, but I feel exhausted and tell Maria that I must go. She looks sad, but says that we shall meet again.
> "Don't worry, Richie. . . . May merciful God take care of you."

I have never forgotten this brief spiritual encounter with my only sister. Those few moments spent in talking with her were for me a turning point, and at the same time an inspiration for and a promise of happiness in the future.

Maria was living in Poland at that time, in our town of Lutsk, as I found out about fifteen years later. It was soon after the start of the German campaign against Russia, and many thousands of troops in mechanized vehicles of various descriptions were rolling across the province of Volhynia, including the town of Lutsk, eastbound. All members of my family have survived that campaign, but they lived through many blood-chilling experiences, in which their very lives were under constant threat.

I drew from that meeting, as if from the horn of plenty, virtually unstoppable desire and strength to survive, to live and prosper. I gained from it an inexhaustible faith in people, in myself, and in life itself.

14
Return to the Land of the Living

Dr. Bronikowski told me that I had slept two days and two nights nonstop. He explained to me later that there were several contagious diseases in that military field hospital, such as dysentery, typhoid fever, malaria, and scurvy. There were no separate wards for any one disease. Any patient brought into any hospital room was exposed to all the diseases that were raging in the hospital at that time, in addition to whatever disease he or she had coming in. There were only one doctor and very few nurses on the hospital staff, all former political convicts in the hard labor camps. They cared for hundreds of victims of several widely ranging epidemics.

Doctor B. told me when I got better that he had absolutely no medicines for the patients and thus aspirin, half-strength (mixed with flour), was all he could prescribe. Whether the patient had typhoid fever, dysentery, or scurvy, the main cure, or illusion of a cure, was five or ten grains of aspirin. Now I also found out about my singing and hallucinations. The doctor also told me that I did a good job of entertaining the patients and staff with my singing.

As it turned out, I had been running a fever of 104 to 106 degrees before I passed the crisis stage in my fight with the diseases, mainly the typhoid fever and double pneumonia. It was thanks to my basically strong physical constitution, especially my strong heart, that I withstood the fever and survived. According to the doctor, the high body temperatures actually helped to kill off the diseases.

My life was hanging on a very thin thread, ready to enter the state of Eternal Happiness at any moment. My soul had knocked at St. Peter's gates, singing all those songs and psalms, begging the Heavenly Doorman to allow me in for a permanent rest, but evidently the Wise Master had other plans for me. He didn't want me up there yet. For several days my body struggled, and it finally won the great battle.

The mortality rate in the hospital was more than 75 percent of all patients admitted. Every day the orderlies carried cold bodies to the common grave, without any official record being kept of the dead. There was insufficient staff to satisfy the needs of patients while they were alive, so those who died did not even get counted.

When I got past the crisis and the high fever, I was transferred to a convalescent center in the nearby village of Kenimeh. It was only a few miles away. I was carried out of the hospital on a stretcher, to a light military truck. I was too exhausted to get up and walk.

The village of Kenimeh was treeless, barren, and deathly hot (100 to 105 degrees in the summer). There was a perpetual state of drought. When water was brought in, probably from the Jangi-Jul River, it was in steel drums, and it tasted brackish, sometimes rusty. We had no choice but to drink it.

I met several interesting individuals in that halfway house. There were perhaps fifty to seventy-five people in the convalescence home, all former patients from the Kermine hospital. They were put five or six men in each room. What we needed most was good food and rest; time would do the healing. Unfortunately, food was scarce, and there was hardly any meat or other form of protein. We received a small piece of bread and soup daily. The soup had a few circles of fish fat on the surface and occasional grains of barley or rice to chase each other across the plate.

I had apparently won the bout with dysentery and typhoid fever; however, I still must have had many unhealed wounds inside me, for I had bad pains in my chest and over most of my body, inside and out. The worst pain was in my lungs. It may have been scarred lung, and other tissues, by the high fever that I had gone through. The doctor told me to eat as much as possible, especially foods rich in fats and proteins. I needed those nutrients, he said, to rebuild my scarred lung and intestinal tissues. That was a good suggestion, I had no doubt about that, but very unrealistic, since we got hardly any fat or protein in our diet. Where could I get a piece of meat?

I wasn't alone in that condition. There were thousands of men and women who had survived the atrociously cruel treatment in the camps in northern Siberia and would very likely have survived many more months in that Arctic freezer. But in the sunny south, various bacteria and epidemics thrived as though nurtured in an incubator. Hundreds of thousands of former prisoners fell victim to many raging epidemics.

15
Bronek's Story

While in the convalescent center, I befriended a young Polish officer, Lt. Bronislaw Szczesny. He was recuperating from a recent and difficult struggle with a series of diseases, just like I had gone through. Lieutenant Szczesny came to sunny Uzbekistan via an interned officers' camp in northwestern Soviet Russia. He told me the story of his experiences, and they horrified me, even though I myself had seen the inside of the hell that is the Soviet slave system. He told me his story in bits and pieces over the period of a few weeks that we had spent together.

The lieutenant was twenty-four years old. He came from the town of Kowel in the southwestern portion of the Volhynia province of eastern Poland. Even though he was just a few years older than I, his face was dried and wrinkled from a long period of starvation and hardships. This made him look at least forty-five to fifty years old. Bronek, as he let me call him, was anxious, actually desperate, to survive. Through several weeks of talking and hunting for scraps of food together, we developed an intimate, almost brotherly relationship of complete trust and confidence in each other. Bronek talked eagerly about his experiences in the internment camps for Polish officers, and about his long journey from the camps in northwestern Russia to Kazakhstan in the south.

He pleaded with me to promise him that I would tell his story to whoever might be interested, should fate not allow him to survive, if ever I got a chance to leave that God-forsaken land alive. Here is Bronek's story as I have reconstructed it.

I was wounded by the Germans in September 1939, near the city of Lvov in southeastern Poland. I was taken to the home of a railroad worker. His family took good care of me, and I soon recovered from my wounds.

When the large masses of Soviet troops arrived in Poland, carrying with them huge posters declaring friendship with the Polish people, thousands of people lined the streets to greet the victorious Soviet army, which "saved" Poland from savage German atrocities. In a few days, the Soviet military high command issued orders for all former military units to lay down their arms and equipment. The Soviet secret police started hunting for all unattached Polish officers. Somebody informed the Soviet authorities of my presence in the railroadman's home. Soon I was arrested by Soviet troops and imprisoned in the town of Stanislavov.

In prison I met a group of Polish men, with whom I would spend two years in various Soviet prisons and camps, even beyond Artiemovsk (in the far north–central part of the USSR). Most of our group of thirteen men were caught in the middle of October 1939, while attempting to cross the Soviet border, to come to the Soviet side. Our goal was to cross the Rumanian boarder, and eventually to make our way to France, where we intended to continue our fight against the Germans. That was after the first phase of the Polish-German war had ended. Among our group of thirteen there were three civilians: an engineer, a judge, and a horse breeder. The remaining ten were all military officers and NCOs. We had hoped not to get caught by the Soviets, having already heard about the mass transportation of Polish military men and civilians into the Soviet Union. We had planned to return to the German-occupied part of Poland, and from there to go south, across the Rumanian-Polish border. Via Rumania,

Bulgaria, and Yugoslavia, we hoped to get to France and Great Britain, where the war with Germany was just starting.

From the Stanislavov prison we were transported through the towns of Lvov, Kiyev, Stalinov, Donbas, Kharkov, and Voroshilov to Starobielsk. We arrived there after several weeks of almost steady traveling, without ever leaving the train.

The Soviet prosecutor at Stanislavov had ordered us to be taken to the Starobielsk internment camp, but the Soviet camp commandant at Starobielsk declared that he was not bound by the orders of the Stanislavov prosecutor, and refused to accept the thirteen of us into his camp. He ordered that we be put back on our cattle train and returned to Stanislavov in Poland.

It was a jurisdictional dispute, no doubt, and each man considered himself in the more important position and able to checkmate the other. The prosecutor at Stanislavov decided to stand by his original decision, and on March 23, 1940, again ordered us to be shipped to Starobielsk, a distance of over five hundred miles from Stanislavov. On the way to Starobielsk for the second time, we only got as far as Artiemovsk, in western Russia. We were taken off the train and locked up in the Artiemovsk prison.

We were kept in that prison from May 1940 until October 1941, approximately seventeen months. The conditions were subhuman. There were twenty-six men in a cell that measured about ten feet by ten feet. We had to sit squatting down, next to each other. Most of the prisoners were Poles. We weren't given access to any news, so we had no idea of what was happening in the outside world. One source of occasional news was the scraps of newspapers that were used as toilet paper by prisoners from other cells. We were let out to the toilet twice a day, at appointed times. We rescued scraps of Russian newspapers, gently washed off the wipings, and thus got at least fractional glimpses of the news.

When, in the summer of 1941, the German-Russian war broke out, nobody told us anything about it. The only signs by which we recognized that a war must have been started again were when the guards were greatly increased in the hallways and the lights were dimmed at night. When we asked the guards if there was a war with the Germans, they told us angrily, "We crushed your country in three days; we'll annihilate the Germans in five."

On the second day of August 1941, a prosecutor visited us in the prison cell. He asked each prisoner what he was in for. I became angry and snapped at him, "I was shooting at your friends, the Germans. That's why I'm in here."

"The Germans were never our friends," the prosecutor answered brusquely, "but all of your people were sold out by your Polish Minister Beck, and that is why you're sitting here."

It was not until September when we found out, from the toilet scraps, that a Polish army was being formed. Mr. Kot was the Polish ambassador to the Soviet Union, and he was making arrangements, on behalf of General Sikorski, for our release from the camp. We waited patiently from day to day for a change. We only hoped, with mixed emotions, that the rapidly advancing German army would make it impossible for the guards to evacuate us. We didn't think that the Artiemovsk prison authorities would leave everything behind but the prisoners.

One day the guards led us out, and put us in formations of four to a line, in total about a thousand people. They issued about a one-kilogram loaf of bread and one salted fish to each of us, and ordered us to march. We left the prison yard surrounded by the 207th convoy regiment, some on foot, some on horses, with the support of a team of dogs. There were eighty women in the convoy. One of them was a Polish woman from Lvov, apparently a prostitute by profession.

As we walked through the streets of Artiemov we encountered some sympathetic people standing alongside the streets. They threw pieces of bread to certain prisoners, who were apparently their friends or relatives. On both sides of the street a great number of women were running alongside our heavily guarded column. Some tried to get inside the prisoners' column when they thought they saw either relatives or loved ones. The guards beat them off with their rifle butts and shoved them away. Our march continued for several hours through the wet, muddy streets. At dusk we came to a hill and the guards gathered us together in a tight group and allowed us to sit down. We received neither food nor drink. One of the Russian prisoners asked for water.

"Here's water for you," answered one of the mounted guards, starting to lash the poor convict with his sword. We not only got no water that day, but we got none the next day either. One of the convoy commanders anounced that if only 5 percent of the prisoners in the convoy reached the destination, it would be more than enough. I was terribly thirsty. I took a piece of bread that I had hidden and chewed on it for several minutes, but I could not swallow it because I didn't have enough saliva to help the food down. My saliva had become white and thick.

The dogs were used by the guards from the first day. The guards did not let the dogs off their leases, otherwise they might have bitten the prisoners to death, but the guards let the dogs closely follow those prisoners who lagged behind. The dogs tore at the clothes of the convicts who slowed down because they either didn't want to or could not keep up with the column's pace. The poor wretches had to marshal all of their strength and continue on.

After a continuous march from 10:00 A.M. until 6:00 P.M., the guards ordered a rest. They told us to sit down, and still gave us no food or drink. We sat, pushed together in a tight group, until sunrise the next morning. It was a bitterly cold night, and it started to rain before sunrise. In the morning we were ordered up on our feet and the march continued.

We were thirsty and the hunger was painful. The remainder of the bread I had wouldn't go down my throat. I was losing strength and falling behind. The saliva was drying up in my throat. We marched through mud, so we carried several pounds of mud clinging to our shoes. Black flakes began to whirl around in front of my eyes. I fell down. I lay there, totally unable to move.

When I came to I got up and Lieutenant Vladek came up to me and helped me along. He gave me a few lumps of sugar, which he squirreled away as a survival ration, for emergencies. The sugar temporarily restored my strength. The black flakes disappeared, and with Vladek's help I began to march again. He saved my life.

The Russian prisoners marching with us were easily divided into two categories. The majority of them were the hoodlum type. They were a tightly knit, insensitive and extremely cruel group. They terrorized the rest of the prisoners. On the second day of our march, these Russian-style gangsters converged on a group of other Russian prisoners and forcibly took from them everything of value, including food and extra clothing. They also took from my hand the last piece of bread I had. The guards didn't react to these strong-arm tactics of one group of prisoners against the other. The existence of dissension among the various groups of convicts assured the guards of very little chance of any conspiracy or insurrection.

In the second group were people with light, short sentences for social crimes, such as being late for work once or twice, even by only fifteen or twenty minutes. Crimes of this type were often punished with sentences of two or three years in labor camps. Some of these men had only a few days left of their sentence before they were due to be released. Now they were told that they would be released at the point of destination—near Stalingrad, about five hundred miles from where we started.

At ten o'clock it began to snow. This was a great joy for us, because we could pick up the snowflakes to quench our thirst. That day we walked about twenty-five miles. At night the guards let us go to a "collective" of buildings, where some of us slept in a school building. Others slept in the hallways of other buldings in the complex. We found out that a couple of days earlier a similar transport of prisoners, also consisting of about a thousand people, had passed through that location. They were from the same Artiemovsk prison.

About sixty-five prisoners were stuffed into a room that measured about seven by eight yards. In the room next door, slightly larger, were about one hundred people. Again, we received neither food nor drink. Only ten men at a time were allowed to go outside to relieve themselves. There was no toilet available, so the men used the floor by the door. The feces were piled ankle-high.

That night, one man died in our room, the first death in our transport. It was a Polish citizen, a Jew. It was a case of heart failure. Another man, a Russian, was shot in the attic, where he was trying to hide. He was brought down, wounded, and dumped on the ox-driven cart. He died at our next stop. At that stop the guards brought a few pails of water into our building. Right away there was a vicious scramble and a stampede for the water. Not even one pail reached our room.

On the fifteenth of August, at about 11:00 A.M., the guards told us to get out into the iced-up yard. They were going to issue bread outside, he said. It was a sunny, but frosty day. Most of the prisoners went out; a few Poles and Ukrainians stayed in. I also stayed in with the other Polish officers. At first I got up and prepared to go out, but all of a sudden, as if by a distant premonition, I sat and told the officer in charge of the Polish group that I wasn't going out. Twice he pleaded with me, for the sake of all that was dear and sacred to us, to make another effort, to get out and get the bread while it was being issued. But I knew that once I got out, the guards would put me in a row, let the dogs out on us, and make us march.

I could see through the window that each man received a

small piece of bread, about two hundred grams, but I didn't move. I was resolved, for I sensed that something would happen to me. After most of the men had left, the guards started beating the backs of the remaining prisoners with their rifle butts and throwing them outside. When I didn't get up after being struck, the guard caught me by the collar of my jacket and dragged me about fifteen yards to the doorway and out into the hall. I hit my head on the doorstep; then I bit my lip to make it bleed. The guard, seeing the blood coming out of my mouth, just said, "He'll rot here." He gave another shove to my chest with his rifle butt and left me there.

In the hallway and in the rooms there were other men lying about, helpless, motionless, resigned to everything. Some were still alive, breathing faintly, but showing no signs of movement. Others were obviously dead, with their tongues hanging out of their mouths as if in a desperate attempt to catch one more breath. Some had their eyes bulging out, with fright and agony frozen in their pain-distorted faces.

As for me, I felt better while lying there than I had felt for a while. I felt no more fear, just a dull sense of pain and a numb sense of gratitude for being left alone. I knew that this was the only way to save myself. Of course, if I had not been determined to lie still, the guards would have forced me to march along with others, and I am sure that I would not have lasted for very long.

The column was formed and the group, now reduced by at least three dozen men, started marching again. For the remaining thirty-odd men, among them fourteen Poles, eight convoy guards stayed behind.

About 1:00 P.M. we heard what sounded like distant artillery shots. We thought it was light artillery at the front line; that perhaps the Germans were pushing forward, which might mean our release may come soon. It turned out to be only antiaircraft artillery.

The remaining prisoners waited one day for further orders or disposition. Finally the guards got word that a freight train was available. In the evening they took all of us out of the building, gave each of us about two hundred grams of bread, and marched us to the railroad station. The guards found an empty wagon, ordered us inside, and locked the doors. They told us the train was on its way to Stalingrad. We started moving east that evening. We had no food beyond the bread ration, because it had all been sent with the major part of our group that went in the same direction by foot. The tracks were all filled with military and war material-related traffic, and there was a general shortage of locomotives. Besides myself there were three other Poles from our original count of thirteen.

We traveled in freight cars or on flatbed cars, which had special barbed-wire walls built around their sides. One time we were put into a wagon filled with barrels of cucumbers. We made a hole in one of the barrels and feasted on cucumbers. We knew that it was better than no food at all. We were not getting any bread rations. Another time we ate a lot of raw corn that local people threw at us from fields located on both sides of the railroad. At the Lichaya station we stopped for five or six days, and there too the local people showed a great deal of sympathy. Sometimes they even threw pieces of dried bread to us. The guards allowed us to get water wherever it was available. We survived largely because of the convoy guards' help, some of whom were stealing food for us from trains and depots we encountered. The guards' orders to deliver us alive were not so absolute, because at one stop the guards got drunk and some of them started shooting blindly at the side of a locked train. A stray bullet hit one of our Polish friends in the head and killed him instantly. One of our fellow prisoners remarked, "There ought to be an investigation of such senseless, wanton killing." He was just being ironic, so we said nothing.

They left the corpse on the train through the night. In the morning they removed the body, and that was that.

After a few days at the Lichaya station our hooligan fellow convicts stole a certain quantity of wheat and rye grain, unground and unprocessed. They were quite generous and gave us some of it, which we gladly accepted. With the lack of food and with hunger pains gnawing at our stomachs, we anxiously devoured those grains. Again, it was much better than nothing and it helped us survive.

We had had nothing warm in our stomachs since we left the Artiemovsk prison. The diet of cucumbers and raw grains caused severe, bleeding diarrhea in all of us. Three men died of diarrhea in my presence, near Stalingrad—all were Polish prisoners. One of them, Dr. L., explained to us just before he died that without at least warm water for over a month, a serious stomach gastritis will result.

On or about November 22, we were let out of our wagon and transported by a light truck to a barrack about eight miles outside the city of Stalingrad. The next afternoon the first group from the Artiemovsk prison arrived. They came the last sixty-five miles by freight train, as they could no longer walk.

One of the Russians from that group recognized me from the beginning of the transport and said, "You were lucky. All your people have perished."

Then each of them repeated the same story, that all the Poles died on the way and there were no Poles in their group now. We could not believe it. The next day the second group of prisoners from Artiemovsk arrived. They were literally shoved into a barrack that measured twenty-two by twelve yards. Two adjacent barracks were assigned to the two groups, which originally consisted of one thousand people each. Between the two groups there, not more than 550 people who survived. They didn't even look human. After their arrival there were ten to twelve deaths daily in our barracks. None of those people had on boots, just rags *wrapped around their legs. The temperatures were in the minus-twenties Centigrade. Their eyes were sunken, almost invisible. Their faces were covered with beards, cheeks dried up, as if they had no flesh. They, like us, had not washed for over a month. When they settled down in the barrack, there was a terrible stench. Most of them had suffered from frostbite, and now the open sores, unattended, were beginning to rot.*

On the first day I was looking for news about the Polish men. There was a young NCO, who was displaying all the symptoms of losing the control of his mind. He was shoeless, with frostbitten legs, and he shivered constantly. I asked him about some of the other men who were with him, and he just kept repeating, "I am cold, I am cold, I am cold."

I asked other convicts about some of our Polish friends. They all had the same answer: "They're all lost."

I asked dozens of people about the fate of our close friends. From their answers, I was able to piece together this story:

The biggest number of people perished during the march across the steppes between the Don and the Volga rivers. One day the whole column had reached a certain place about fifty miles from a collective farm. The guards ordered a rest, since the marchers were all totally exhausted. There was a large corral for the cows, a saray *the Russians called it. We spent five very cold days and five nights in this corral. They gave us no food.*

The convicts broke the wooden fences to make a fire. The hoodlum prisoners sat in a tight ring around the fire, and let no one near it, especially the Polish prisoners, who were generally weaker and a small minority. The Poles, for the most part, had better, warmer clothes, so the hoodlums forced the Poles to undress and took their clothes away from them, leaving them sometimes only in their shirt and underpants.

On the sixth day the guards brought some horsemeat, cooked a soup for the convicts, and distributed a cupful of meat to each. Then they ordered us to march on. Sixty men refused to go. The guards called those sixty to the side and the convoy commander told them to go to a nearby well to get some water for themselves. The commander ordered those who went for water to join the ranks and march on. Fourteen out of sixty refused to go even for water. The fourteen were led behind a little house on the farm and a salvo of shots was heard in a few minutes. Immediately, the other prisoners rushed behind the house and stripped the bodies of their clothes.

The convoy started marching again. Everyday now there were casualties. Men were dropping dead or refusing to march on, after which the guards shot them without hesitation. When we reached the destination, the guards checked the prisoners' names for a whole week. There were no statistics kept, and even the names of the dead ones were not registered anywhere. When a person whose name was called did not respond, the other prisoners shouted, "Died," or "Stayed in the corral."

For the first two weeks in the barracks we received three hundred grams (about ten ounces) of bread daily and two or three pails of water were brought into the barracks.

The bread was usually issued outside. The men stood in line, and each got a slice. We Poles ate our bread rations outside, before we got back into the barracks, otherwise the hoodlums grabbed the bread from the weaker men who still had it in their hands.

One day the guards didn't lead us outside for the issuance of the bread rations. They gave it to us in the barracks. We were told to sit up on our sleeping shelves while the guards gave out the bread. In the passage, a man was lying on the floor, in the final stages of dying. He was already stripped of his clothes by his comrades. His eyes were closed and he made strange motions with his arms and legs. One of the guards made a remark. "He doesn't need bread anymore. He's going to die soon anyway."

The guards hesitated for a moment, wondering what he was going to do with the dying man's bread ration. He held a slice of dark rye in his right hand, taunting them. Right away, several men threw themselves at the bread, stomping all over the dying man. He passed away within a half hour.

There was always a shortage of water. We picked up snow outside, brought it in, and ate it. Some resourceful men did good business on the snow; they carried it in on a rag, melted it, and sold it for bread.

In certain places on the field near the barracks some strange-looking posts were sticking out of the snow. As we went closer, we recognized them as dead, naked prisoners. The guards apparently were dragging the dead bodies out of the barracks across the snow-covered field into a mass grave. From then on we avoided that part of the field in our search for snow.

Every night we heard strange moaning noises in the barracks. We soon found out that some of the weaker convicts, who were in the final stages of dying, were actually being choked by their neighbors. They wanted to strip them of their clothes as soon as possible, so they could sell their clothes for bread. Every morning several dead naked bodies were taken out of the barracks.

After a few days, the Polish prisoners decided to band together for mutual protection. We all gathered in one part of the barrack, to sleep in one group.

The sleeping shelves were arranged in two or three tiers, to accommodate more people in the barrack. At first we slept on the top shelf, thinking that might be safer. But soon we saw that some of our group were too weak to climb to the top tier, or to come down from it. So we decided to move to the bottom shelf at floor level. In the bottom tier there were only about twenty inches of space between the floor and the second tier. Some of us had to crawl, on elbows and knees, to sleeping spots in the back. We slept four abreast in our space, with the strongest two on the outside, so as to put up a more defensive stand against the hoodlums' assaults and attempts to rob us of whatever we had. The conditions of our Polish group improved tremendously after we formed a common camp. The hoods didn't attack us with the impunity that they had before.

From about the first of December 1941, my health began to worsen. I lost my appetite. I couldn't even eat the daily bread ration. I could no longer swallow the salty fish, I felt feverish, had pain in my lungs, and my mouth was full of raw sores, which made swallowing painful and difficult.

From the first days of December the guards started calling out Polish names. Many people whose names were called were no longer with us, but if the person being called answered, the guard would say, "Sobierayties' z vieshchami [get ready, with your belongings]."

On the eleventh day of December, I heard my name called. The guard said to me, "Sobierayties' z vieshchami," and I forgot about being tired and weak. I got up quickly and in a few minutes I was standing at the door. One or two remaining Polish friends pleaded with me to remember them.

I was taken to the camp's office. They gave me a two-kilogram (five-pound) loaf of bread, one kilogram of salted fish, forty-five rubles, sand then the commissar said that I was now a Soviet Grazhdanin (citizen), and a free man.

On the way out I almost fell from being very weak, and from the effect of the strong emotions which I felt were overcoming me. One of the guards at the gate told me which way I should go to get to the railroad station for a train going to Stalingrad. From Stalingrad I was to go to the city of Kuybishev, where the Polish embassy was located.

At the Polish embassy I met with the utmost assistance and also had a couple of good meals. The people at the embassy were very friendly and anxious to help all Polish citizens. My strength gradually began to come back to me, very slowly. I received an official confirmation now that there was a Polish army being formed at Buzuluk near Kuybyshev in the Ukraine.

I received more money and food supplies, and was told to

head on to Buzuluk. I had lost all hope of surviving much longer, but I wanted at least to die among friends, who would show me sympathy, understanding, and friendship.

Thus ended Bronek's story.

16
May They Rest in Peace

The days passed. Our daily food rations were not enough to sustain us. Bronek and I made trips around the village of Kenimeh and into the countryside on the outskirts of the village. We looked around for plants and animals that could be edible. Sometimes we caught fairly large turtles and found roots of certain wild-growing plants, such as horse carrot and parsley root. The cleaning women in our convalescent center made these into soups for us. They had good meals themselves out of our efforts. We had a hard time killing the poor turtles, because they kept hiding inside their hard shells. We had to wait quietly until the turtle extended its head and legs to resume its cautious forward march, so that one of us could grab its head and the other could quickly hack it off with a knife. Once the turtle was killed it was easy to quarter and make ready for cooking. Sometimes we had to cook the turtles ourselves in a pot on an open fire in the field. The turtle meat and the soup made out of it were delicious, the taste resembling very closely the best chicken meat. But the texture of the meat was very tough, so we had to cook it for several hours to make it edible. Horse and camel meat were also very tasty, but very difficult to come by. It was even harder to cook them to make them soft enough to eat.

Lieutenant Bronek and I shared many interesting expeditions and experiences in the few weeks we spent together. While we did various things together, or just roamed around the countryside, Bronek continued telling me of his gruesome struggle for survival during his trek south from central European USSR.

Our daily struggle to survive and to get food, in addition to what we were getting at the convalescent house, kept us busy. At the convalescent home our daily rations of food were barely sufficient to keep us alive, but certainly not for us to feel well or get stronger. We were still sick and very weak, so we couldn't be very effective, since there was not much food available anywhere in the whole area. But we kept on trying.

One day, in the late afternoon, Bronek and I were roaming around the village. I usually carried a knife with me, in case we encountered some roots or plants in the field that looked edible. We had learned to recognize, by appearance, smell, or touch, which plants or roots might be beneficial to us. That afternoon we hadn't been very lucky in finding edible plants.

Then we both saw a medium-size dog walking aimlessly around, looking into holes in the ground and around the bushes. I don't know even now who spoke out first, Bronek or I, but our thoughts ran close together. We looked at the dog, kind of lean, short hair, short tail, about eighteen inches high, and then we looked at one another.

The question we saw in each other's eyes was, *Why not him?* And both of us unanimously answered, *Why not?* Perhaps we had come across an answer to our problem of getting nutritional food. We were both desperately craving some meat; it made no difference then what kind of meat. The decision was simple. Neither one of us had to justify anything to the other.

We gently lured the dog near us and petted it, until it was lying down. Then I told Bronek to hold the dog's front legs and muzzle, and I put my knees on its hind legs, with its belly up.

The whole process of killing the poor innocent animal was quite gruesome, especially without having proper tools for such a job. I still have not quite forgiven myself for committing such a distasteful deed. In those circumstances, however, and at that time it seemed excusable that one had to kill to ensure one's own survival. When the animal was dead, Bronek went to our house to get a container from the cleaning woman, who also worked as a helper in the kitchen. I had most of the skin separated by the time he returned.

We threw the bottom part of the front legs, all of the hind legs, and the guts, except the heart, into a cluster of bushes nearby. The last thing we had to think about was how and where to cook it.

When we brought our prized possession to our convalescent home, we first talked to the woman who lent us the container, Mrs. Sowa. We told her it was a piece of mutton that we had gotten from an Uzbek. We suggested that she cook it for us, for which she would share the meat with us.

The women in the kitchen made a large pot of soup, with seasonings and vegetables, whatever they could find in the kitchen. It was delicious, and they all had their share out of it. I don't know if they really thought it was mutton, but nobody said anything about it tasting unusual. It is said, "Beggars can't be choosers." The Polish equivalent saying is, "Darowanemu koniowi nie zagląda się w zęby," which means, in loose translation, "One shouldn't be checking the age of a horse one is getting for free."

There were three other men in the ward where my friend Bronek and I stayed. They all had a good helping of the rich, nutritious broth and a nice piece of well-cooked meat. Bronek enjoyed a couple of good full meals out of that. Unfortunately, Bronek felt quite sick after eating those meals. The next two days he felt progressively worse, and he had to be taken back to the hospital at Kermine. About a week later I heard the sad news that Bronek had died. Apparently, that meat and the soup were too rich in animal fat to be digested by his devastated, delicate gastric system.

I felt bereft, angry, even guilty. I thought I had, at least partially, contributed to Bronek's sickness and death. I went to confession and had a good talk with the priest, who granted me absolution from any guilt in this case. He said that since my intention was to help him and the other people, I could not conscientiously blame myself for such a negative outcome. I thought often about Bronek, however. Why was such a young and promising life destroyed before its time? Why were so many millions of faintly flickering stars snuffed out of their orbits just as they were perhaps ready to lend their light to others, to help them see better? I asked the heavenly Master then and many times since, *Why?* Especially at the point when Bronek was at the threshold of a new kind of life? He could have enjoyed many things in life, and could perhaps have done many good things. My mind worked through many such sad, philosophical thoughts, but eventually I had to relegate such thinking to its proper perspective. I decided that everyone had to fulfill his responsibility first for himself and his own life. I couldn't allow any such thoughts to hinder my chances of making progress in my own current life. I had witnessed and lived through the deaths of many friends, of many who had become dear to me. Suffering and death had become a normal part of my life. I had learned to recognize the sad fact that everyone had their Final Hour to respond to our Creator's call. Until then, we have to keep on going, and to try our best to cope with life's problems.

In a few weeks' time of my staying at the convalescent home I had gained a little weight, and I began to feel healthier. All around me in the convalescent home, people were coming and going. The daily death rate was still about 50 percent of the incoming patients. Every day I saw bodies wrapped in white sheets, being carried out to a common grave.

One day, as I was on one of my frequent searches, this time at the outskirts of the city, I heard a faint voice calling my name. I didn't recognize the voice, but when I looked at the boy who was calling me, I saw it was Thad Lubek, the policeman's son from my town of Lutsk, back in the Volynia. He was lying on a blanket spread on sandy grass. I could see right away Thad was still very sick and exhausted. He had been ill with typhoid fever and dysentery and had gone through the hospital at Kermine, he told me. He had recovered enough to be released from the hospital, but he wasn't well, not by far.

I sat with Thad on the sandy field. Around us were scattered clumps of miserly growing grass that looked like it had not been thriving well either. Men were carrying a dead body, about thirty feet from us, to a common grave. That funeral process didn't register very strongly on my consciousness, because at that moment my mind had gone blank. I didn't feel any reaction in me.

Thad was glad to see me, because he had long been separated from the rest of our group. He was the boy who denounced me during the interrogations at the NKVD headquarters and later in the prison. At that time, and for some months afterwards, I had felt quite angry about what he had done to us all. Later, however, my anger at him subsided, because I had to cope with too many problems every day—those were urgent problems of survival and they somehow drowned all the petty angers. Now, seeing Thad so helpless and needing a friendly hand, I felt no anger at all. He was weaker than I, and I wanted to help him. Since the People's Court session, when we were sentenced to various periods of slavery in the labor camps, Thad had been transferred through some three or four camps in north-central Siberia. His mind must have been affected by his experiences, because he was not quite coherent, and his eyes didn't focus well. He kept looking around, as if he were scared of somebody. I tried to talk to him about our distant past, about the good times we had together at Rogova Street in Lutsk, about our neighbors, the Gonchakovskis, who lived in a beautiful house on a hill and whose son gave such captivating violin concerts from the hilltop. I said to Thad, "Do you remember the beautiful girl Helen Braun, the mailman's daughter?"

He just mumbled something, weakly, incoherently, that sounded like, "Yes, I do, they went to Germany. They were Volkdeutsches." It surprised me that he remembered that much, because he couldn't tell me much else. He didn't seem to remember about the most recent events of his experiences at Kenimeh, or even the bad beating he survived from the big sailor.

It was dinnertime. I suggested that we should go to the dining hall to get our food. Thad said, in a very weak voice, that he didn't feel well, and would rather stay where he was. So I said I would bring his dinner.

I went to the dining hall, stood in line, and asked for two portions, saying that my friend (I mentioned his name) didn't feel well and had asked me to bring his dinner to him. The cook knew Thad as one of the new arrivals, and he let me take two bowls of rice with some meat flavor in it. I enjoyed the curried aroma of it and ate my portion, which tasted good. When I looked at Thad, however, he was picking at the individual grains of rice in his bowl, with waning energy in his movements.

Seeing Thad's lack of enthusiasm for eating his dinner, I offered to help him. He seemed indifferent to the idea of eating. I talked to him about our mutual experiences in Lutsk, the trips on the River Styr, the expeditions we had made to the underground tunnels in Count Lubart's Castle and the Cathedral in Lutsk, and the fun we had had on the ice. Thad responded to these memories, but without showing any lively interest, as if there was only a mild awakening of his consciousness. His eyes seemed better focused, temporarily, when I talked about those things of the past. Then I could even see a very slight twitching in his eyes, as if an emotion was welling up right from the depths of his soul, or his eyes were ready to issue forth some tears. These changing moods of his inner soul were faintly noticeable in his eyes, which were gazing into the far distances up above in the skies. There were occasional minute twitches moving across his face. But, alas, his whole system was too much weakened to provide the energy required to set these feelings in motion.

I continued giving him small half-spoonfuls of rice, which he accepted more to please me than to eat. I talked about the surrounding barren flat land and the small hills near the horizon. His head was resting in my lap and he seemed peaceful. In certain moments his face showed both the pain and joy that were alternating in his soul. He spoke very weakly, "They have destroyed us."

I tried to cheer him up. "Thad, maybe not quite. Don't worry. You'll be all right. We'll go back to Lutsk together."

"No," he said, "not I. When you go there, tell my mother I was thinking about her. I miss her."

"Yes, Thad. We'll both tell her together."

As I fed him more rice, he started getting heavier on my lap. I raised a spoonful of rice to his mouth, but his lips didn't open. His eyes became stationary, looking out into space, without any expression in them. His breathing slowed down to almost nothing, then he gave out a very faint sigh, his last. I closed his eyes, put his head gently on the blanket, and said a short prayer for his soul.

"God, if You are up there, please hear me out. My friend here, Thad, had a very hard and painful life on this earth. Grant him, please, O Lord, a peaceful rest by Your side. If he hurt my case at NKVD interrogations through his weakness or his carelessness, I hereby declare I hold no more grudge against him. I fully forgive him."

I don't know what the good Judge did with Thad, but I thought Thad had suffered and atoned sufficiently for any sins of weakness he may have committed in his life.

Another friend, another death, I thought. I began to wonder who was going to be the next one in line. Slowly, after sitting for some length of time, I got up, slightly dizzy, and drained of all emotions.

I went back to the house to tell the orderlies of another body lying in the field. Then I went out again in another direction, just to be alone. Out in the open field, I sat on a ridge beside a desert bush, and had a very sad time, alone. I felt like crying, but I was too sad to cry. I guess I had gotten out of the habit of crying. Life just didn't seem right, but as I thought and looked around me, I saw no one else who appeared better off than I. I dozed off by the bush, in a half-stupor, a half-emptied state of mind.

Later, when I came to, it was twilight. The sun had just set, but I could see quite well where I was, and I could see the convalescent house in the distance. I headed back, because I did not want to be alone any more. On the western horizon the colors of the setting sun were gradually changing from reddish to pale pink. Then pink was replaced by gray and finally it all became dark gray, which left me sad and depressed. It had been a difficult day for me, and I was glad it had ended.

Throughout my entire period of imprisonment, the journey to eastern Siberia, and my experiences in the prison camps, I had maintained a very strong desire to survive. Prior to my imprisonment, I had enjoyed the simple, enriched happiness of living a life in which I was always sure to receive love and affection. I was allowed to enjoy the outdoors to the fullest degree, but I also knew that my family expected me to attend to my obligations at school and chores at home. I had loved life, though I didn't always understand the real sense of it. Now, after losing several very close friends, in such wretched, hopeless circumstances, my will to live had sagged to a very low ebb.

While heading back to my convalescent home, I thought to myself, *What's the sense of this life? Why is it my lot in life to meet people, make friendships, nurture them, become attached to them, and then lose them irretrievably? I have learned to love people and perhaps even to depend on their love and friendship, only to have my best friends snatched away just at the height of my growing attachment to them. Why?*

After each death of a person close to me, I felt less joy in me, less of the willpower and strength to form new attachments, to start life anew. Life had become only a struggle to survive and to supplement the meager rations of food that we were getting from the army kitchens. It meant the rebuilding of the body, so it would be better able to sustain the wilting soul and spirit. In witnessing daily the deaths of people around me, I felt my physical health began to fail. I wasn't sick with any specific illness, but I was losing the will to go on. The meals were the same, but I was no longer anxious to eat them, or to supplement them. Several hundred thousand Polish prisoners in Soviet Russia, military as well as civilians, fought bravely for their lives against the diseases and lost that fight. They were buried in the barren deserts of Uzbekstan and Kazachstan.

A few hundred thousand others who survived the prisons, the labor or the resettlment camps, were lucky enough to be taken out of the Soviet country, and were allowed to see the other side of the world. I had almost succumbed to the epidemics of the typhoid fever and dysentery and after coming out a winner in those fights, I almost missed being put on one of the last one or two transports put together to be taken to the port of Krasnovodsk on the Caspian Sea, and from there to Iran.

By this time several groups of soldiers, a few thousand men and women each, had been shipped west by trucks and trains toward the Caspian Sea. The transports had to go across the Kara Kum Desert. The trip from Samarkand, via Bukhara, and Ashkhabad, to the Soviet port of Krasnovodsk on the Caspian Sea (a distance of about twelve to thirteen hundred kilometers) would take many days. Again, the military commanders and the organizers of these shipments had learned by the experience of their predecessors. They knew that the Kara Kum Desert's heat, reaching well over 105 degrees Fahrenheit, dry and unrelenting, would tax the endurance of even the toughest and healthiest individuals. To the sick and convalescent ones, it was obviously courting complete disaster. It was only the desperation to get these people out of the USSR that finally drove the commanding officers to order everybody loaded on trucks heading west. If the sick had been left behind, there was hardly any doubt that they would not survive long. My physical condition seemed to improve quite satisfactorily and I dreamt of getting out of the convalescent home.

From the Kenimeh convalescent home, most of us were loaded on trucks and driven to Samarkand, where we were reloaded onto a train going west to Bukhara. I had barely enough strength to get onto the truck with someone's help. By the time the train arrived in Bukhara, I had suffered a complete relapse, both physical and emotional. I felt too weak to walk and had lost all interest in what was going on around me. I had completely lost the desire to live anymore. The heat and stifling air in the train had finished me off. When the Red Cross staff met us at the Bukhara station, greeting us with American-made Spam, and Nabisco shortbread cookies to entice our appetite, I didn't feel like eating any food. I had passed the stage of wanting food. I still suffered with a bleeding dysentery and post-typhoid confusion. The Red Cross personnel carried me on a stretcher to the other train, but I was unconscious and unable to cooperate.

From the city of Bukhara the train crossed the Amu-Daria River and a valley of the same name. There must have been about two days' travel across the Kara Kum Desert toward the Elburz mountain chain, which was on the border between the USSR and Iran. My recollection of that trip, however, is vague, because I was feverish and mostly unconscious.

17
Leaving the Land of Slavery—to Iran and Iraq

Our military leaders were getting anxious to close the Polish camps, because the Soviets were more and more unwilling to furnish, both civilian and military personnel, with supplies of food, clothing, and medical needs.

The Soviet authorities were starting other small Polish Army sub-units, attached to Soviet military units and totally under Soviet command. Thus, the Soviet leaders wanted to cut off transports of Polish people out of Soviet territories, in order to resume complete control over the fate of Poles who would be left there. The Soviet government organized a meeting of a small group of Polish communists in Saratov at the beginning of 1943, at which a new, Soviet-sponsored organization was formed under the name of "Alliance of Polish Patriots."

This alliance, directed by the NKVD "inserts," formed a "Committee for National Liberation" in July 1944, in cooperation with a group of communists already active in Poland under the German occupation. The Germans eventually started retreating under heavy attacks of the Soviet armies, strengthened by modern American weaponry and plentiful supplies of foods and ammunitions under the Lend-Lease agreements between the Western Allies and the Soviets. The Soviet armies were by then well supplied with many thousands of able-bodied and well-trained Polish troops taken from groups of survivers of the labor camps and prisons.

The Polish government, in exile in England, in dealing with Stalin (according to the Sikorski-Stalin Agreement, dated July 30, 1941), wanted to have large units of the Polish Army organized, under Polish commanders, on the Russian soil. These Polish brigades were to fight, according to the plans of the Polish leaders, alongside the Russian armies. But the Russians had already formulated other plans—they wanted to scatter the Polish soldiers among the Russian units, so as to have no strong, meaningful concentration of the Polish military strength.

It was unwise (and scary) for the Russians to have the Polish troops, in large units, fully armed, led by their own leaders—all of whom, the soldiers as well as the officers, had just a short time before been ruthlessly invaded, arrested, imprisoned, shot at, and cruelly treated in the death-labor camps, with their families destroyed or dying in the agony of hunger or diseases. Such people could be trusted with arms, but could not be controlled, unless they were interspersed singly or in small, harmless units, among Russian officers, under constant surveillance of the super-efficient spying network instituted in all Russian military units.

When the time came to be fighting on Poland's own territory, such Polish troops would be a constant threat of a rebellion and opposition to the Russian plans of installing their own government, loyal only to Russia, in Poland. Polish officers would not order their own soldiers to disarm and shoot their own brothers and relatives who were fighting in the anti-German underground resistance units of the Home Army (Armia Krajowa). And they wouldn't stand by idly, fully armed, if they saw the Russians doing it. The Russians were fully conscious of such realities.

However, Polish troops under the Soviet command had been used not only to fight the Germans retreating across Poland, but also had the grim assignment to search out and destroy the soldiers of the Polish resistance movement (Armia Krajowa). The units of the Committee of National Liberation were also used to identify the remaining Polish patriots in Poland, who had fought against the German occupational forces, and report them to the Soviet commanders, to be ruthlessly destroyed by special squads in mass executions.

Polish commanders of newly formed military units and the directors of the hospital and convalescent-home complexes did all in their power to get transports organized. Our transport was the next to the last one that made it to Krasnovodsk, before these shipments were stopped altogether by the Soviets.

I was in such a feverish and sickly condition, that I was not in any state of mind to be thinking about all those high-level worldly problems. I do remember the suffocating heat, which was adding to my misery. We arrived at Krasnovodsk after a few days.

The medical orderlies and nurses taking care of a number of bed-ridden, hopeless cases like me took us on stretchers from the train onto a slow-speed freight steamboat. The steamer was an old veteran of the Caspian Sea routes known by the name of *Baku*. The vessel was not much to look at, just a utility cargo ship, doing her job. There were no hospital wards and no hospital beds, although she had performed hospital functions to many thousands of patients. But a miracle happened to me—as soon as we cast off the moorings, I began to feel like a different individual. I changed my mind about wanting to die!

It was certainly a case of spirit over body, because my

will to live returned to me. In the three days and two nights that it took us to travel across a wide stretch of this great inland sea, I was able to get up, eat well, and walk cautiously around the deck. The weather and travel conditions were beautiful. The sun was hot, but the large body of water made it completely bearable. There was hardly a speck of cloud up in the skies. We were approaching freedom; I am sure that made a lot of difference to all of us.

The Iranian port of Pahlevi did not have much of a city around it to support it. There were no skyscrapers, no big buildings. After the disembarkation and head count, we were loaded onto trucks and driven away out of the city, to a sandy area, where there was a separate tent city.

We were driven directly to a military quarantine camp located a good distance from the seashore. It was an area of several square miles, all covered with tents. The stretcher cases were placed in a separate part of the camp, apparently for fear of contagious diseases. The quarantine period was, in most cases, six weeks.

I soon discovered new strength and my energy was fast returning to me. That was attributable to several factors: an atmosphere created where we were sure that we were among friends; the food was plentiful, although controlled by the nurses for our own sakes; and the doctor attending us watched us carefully and checked our vital signs frequently.

Because our whole physical condition and, in particular, our digestive systems had been damaged severely, the medics were especially carefully watching for outbreaks of new epidemics. The epidemics of dysentery and typhoid fever did strike again, however, brought about by new environment and perhaps, ironically, by the ideal climate and plentiful supplies of good food. In the beginning period of three months, a few hundred people were hurriedly buried in the sandy soil of Iran. They were victims of dysentery and typhoid fever.

The medical staff tried to make sure that our shriveled and sickened digestive systems were not damaged more by too much rich food, too soon. Those of us who, by the nurses' judgement, could eat safely without any restrictions were allowed to eat their fill. Plenty of food was available, even though its variety was limited.

The main items on the menu every day was the tender meat of the *caracul*, or Persian lamb. These little animals were killed when they were only a couple of weeks old. To breeders, most of their commercial value was in their skins, which were sold to make astrakhan furs. The meat was only a byproduct, so it was sold or given to the Polish Army units by the Iranians. It was either grilled on an open fire, or cooked in one of several ways by the army cooks. It was deliciously tender and easily digested by even the weakest stomachs. It was served with either rice or with flat cakes made out of plain flour. These cakes were baked on a flat hotplate in the kitchen, or on hot coals by the open fire on the sand.

For breakfast or between meals, for those who needed extra food and could handle it, we could have plenty of eggs. Many times I would devour a dish of up to fifteen eggs scrambled and made to my liking! I just grew in strength and filled out so fast, it was as if I was bread dough and everything I ate had yeast in it. We were also allowed to drink generous amounts of local moonshine, made from rice.

At the end of the quarantine period I passed the medical examinations with flying colors. The following week my name was included on the list of the next transport to Teheran. A large transient camp made up of those who survived the Soviet slavery had been established there for the Polish Army. Now this was a regular army, and I was proud to be wearing the uniform of a regular infantry soldier (Seventh Infantry Division), minus a rifle and some training on how to use it in case of need.

To get to Teheran, we had to cross the Gilan section of the Elburz mountain chain, which has peaks of up to fifteen thousand feet above sea level. Traveling across those mountains in the Persian military trucks was blood chilling. The trucks were driven by hired Persian drivers, civilians who were supposedly the best qualified men to drive across the hazardous serpentine roads. The highway was cut into the slopes of the mountainside. Through the first leg of the journey we were constantly climbing up the mountain. The road led through several ravines and mountain passes, and was extremely dangerous.

There were many sudden and sharp turns, sometimes at about forty-five degree angles, following the ragged and very irregular contours of the mountains. I heard from others, later, that even though those drivers were very experienced and familiar with the roads, they had to be half-drunk to dare driving trucks full of people on those roads. I was placed in the rear part of the truck, almost on the rear board. On several occasions, the driver couldn't make the curve in one try, so he backed up the truck, and then completed the turn. When he backed up, the rear end of the truck was about two feet from the edge of the mountain, with a drop of at least five hundred feet, with no protective wall or fence. My view down below was dizzying because the front end of the truck was tilted slightly upwards. I almost passed out when I saw the remnants of many cars and trucks and other things all down the slope. It was indeed a horrifying experience.

Occasionally we saw various animals running across

the road. There were big rats, the size of rabbits, and lizards with very high front legs, running across the road. It was the most beautiful and the most dangerous road I have ever traveled on. In about two days we were on the other side of the mountain, going down the serpentine roads at high speeds. The rear of the truck was open most of the time, with just a tarpaulin sheet hanging cross the opening, so we couldn't help being awed by the magnificent scenery as well as a good view of the breathtaking hazards we were barely scraping through.

The rest of the trip to Teheran was peaceful, in comparison to the experiences crossing the Elburz mountains. The mountain slopes and peaks looked dry and barren now; it was already autumn.

Our first impressions of the Iranian people were formed in Pahlevi, where we met many Iranians who visited the camps. Those people were extremely kind and compassionate, even generous to us. Our needs were many at that time, but the most urgent and noticeable to anybody who came near us, was the need for food and kindness. The Iranians fulfilled both of those needs wholeheartedly. They supplied lots of food for both the military and civilian camps, as well as for the small number of civilian refugees outside of the camps. The Iranians were anxious to show us their support, solidarity, and sympathy towards us. They knew that we had left the land of misery and fear. Word had gotten to them of our plight and the treatment we had received while in the Soviet Union.

The Soviets at that time occupied the northern part of Iran, and their presence there could be felt in many ways, even in Teheran. The NKVD agents found out that the Iranians began to fraternize with the Polish refugees, the survivors of the Soviet slave system, and that our new hosts, the Iranians, were beginning to show a more antagonistic attitude towards the Soviets, from seeing our tragic condition. The Iranians knew that the raggedy appearance and the deathly physical state of so many thousands of small Polish children was a direct result of the Soviets. The Soviet agents then published several stories in the Persian and Hindu newspapers, telling the Iranians their (the Soviet) version of the truth. According to those stories, it was just the Germans who were brutally mistreating the Polish people, and particularly their children. The Russians did the good deed, by taking these children away from the Germans, and now were shipping them out of the USSR—to place them away from the dangers of war. Even Goebbels, the most famous German master of deceit, could not have produced a more sophisticated lie.

In Teheran, while we were still riding in the trucks, the people, young and old, of both sexes, waved their hands to us with friendly greetings. We stayed in Teheran only for about six weeks. We had physical drills in the morning, to develop and maintain ourselves in good condition, but for most of the day we were free and could get passes to go out on the town. While visiting the city, we were free to go to the marketplaces, public buildings, and some of our men even went to the Shiite Muslim mosques. There were a number of buildings with fine architecture, exquisite mosaic designs, and rich Oriental-style ornaments on the walls and tops of the buildings.

During our sightseeing excursions to the Muslim temples and other public buildings, we saw paintings and statues of the past conquerors of these lands. From these historical relics and from the explanations of the local guides and other people we learned about the cruelty, merciless rapes, and mass killings that occurred every few decades throughout Asia Minor. There were raids and conquests made into Persia between the fourteenth and eighteenth centuries by the Uzbeks, Turkmen, and Afghans. These conquests, followed by mass killings, usually changed whole provinces into barren, uninhabited deserts.

We witnessed many examples of callousness of the local Persian authorities toward the sick and those who were less fortunate among them. There were very rich people, living in castlelike splendor behind well-guarded gates, and mobs of people, just outside, milling around in the crowded streets of the city proper. These people were of many origins and mixtures, some small-featured of Chinese or other Oriental parentage, others broad-faced Mongols, dark-skinned Hindus, or Semitic types like Armenians, and also Kurds or Arabs.

Because of the kindness the Persians had shown to us, we were surprised, while walking around the streets, to see quite a few beggars and sick people begging for alms in whatever form. Women wore mostly dark, long robes, and tight-fitting black veils that covered their entire faces, except for their eyes and foreheads. The women were not very communicative, as if shy or forbidden by custom to speak to strange men. They did manage to express their kindness by gestures and bows, and thus made us feel welcome.

In Teheran we finally found out that our next destination was Iraq. The exact location in Iraq was not known as yet. A number of military trucks were soon made available, under the command of British officers. This overland trip took us about a week. The destination was Baghdad, capital of Iraq.

The journey through the deserts of western Persia, and the Zagras Mountains was long. We also passed through the cities of Hamadan and Kermanshah. We were exhausted when we arrived in Baghdad. There were many small villages along our way, none of which had ever recovered from the various raids of the past centuries. The country was very hilly and there was very little arable land. The people were engaged mostly in raising sheep.

Our stay in Baghdad was brief, just long enough to get the gasoline tanks refilled and some maintenance work done on the trucks. We were given a little time to eat and rest and to walk around the city. The central section of the city was modern, with wide streets and electric streetlights, allowing for motorized traffic. In the middle of the city, in a large square, there was a huge statue of King Faisal, founder of the modern state of Iraq, whose son ruled the country during our stay there. The Germans had been in this area since the beginning of the twentieth century, as evident from horsedrawn vehicles with automobile horns and markings *Made in Germany*. In the open-air bazaars and stores, the merchants displayed a great variety of goods from Asia, Africa, and Europe.

We went on to our destination, which was the small town of Khanaqin, about seventy miles northeast of Baghdad. Our tent camp was situated outside the town on the western slopes of the Zagras mountains, very near the borderline between the Kurdistan and Iraq. In the Khanaqin camp we were again processed through a series of very thorough medical tests, and through tests on literacy and general knowledge.

These tests were not too difficult for me. I passed them with good results and was told that I was now qualified to be accepted by the Polish Air Force. That meant going to Great Britain, which surprised me and made me very happy. The group of us who passed these qualifying exams for the Air Force totaled about five hundred out of this latest transport of men. The rest of the men whose scores were below a certain level were to be shipped to Egypt and to Palestine, there to be enlisted into the Carpathian Brigade. That brigade later fought against the Germans in the Italian invasion, including the taking of the Monte Casino monastery.

Our stay near the little town of Khanaqin was boring. The daily routine consisted of some physical drills in the morning, including marching in unit formations, before breakfast, which was at about 7:00 A.M. Next followed some two to three hours of instructions on military rules and procedures, and English classes, if an instructor was available. The rest of the day was filled up with guard duties, day and night. The temperatures reached 105-110 degrees in the afternoon, but the air was very dry. It was a real desert, high above sea level. Even the sand got so hot that we couldn't touch it with bare feet or hands. By a standing order, which was strictly enforced for our own protection, we had to stay inside the tents between 2:00 and 4:00 P.M. The outside air felt like an oven when we tried to put our face outside the tent. That afternoon break was officially called the "dead hours."

Just on the other side of the hills from where our camp was located were several Kurdish villages. The Kurds had been waging a long-lasting struggle for independence from their neighbors, Iraq and Iran. Kurdistan was split between three countries, Iraq, Iran, and Turkey, all of which were far too rich and powerful for the brave Kurds in an open war. The best the Kurdish national zealots could do was to engage in a fierce constant guerrilla war that lasted for generations. Our temporary campsite fell victim to several Kurdish assaults and frequent harrassments.

I stood guard one night near the hills, and as soon as dusk fell I witnessed a strange phenomenon. Darkness fell quickly after sunset in those regions near the Tropic of Capricorn. Our company had several field guns that were used for drills and military maneuvers. They were left near the hills for the night. As I marched up and down a certain sector assigned to me, I noticed one cannon kept changing its position. Each time I turned around, the cannon appeared to have moved farther away from me, closer to the hills. Originally the cannon had been standing about two hundred feet from my position. Finally, I ran towards the gun, shouted "Halt, who's there?" (in Polish), and fired a warning shot in its direction. It stopped moving. When I approached it, I found a rope attached to the axle of the two-wheel cart carrying the gun. The other end of the rope led up to the hills. A patrol was dispatched immediately to investigate who was behind the hill but, of course, nobody was found. We had several incidents of such sneaky attacks, so the guards were warned to be particularly alert to those tricks.

After all the soldiers in our camp were medically examined and tested for their general knowledge, we were transported south, toward the port of Basra in the Persian Gulf. There was a small ship waiting for us to take us to Bombay, India. Our ship was packed to the brim. In addition to a couple of thousand of our troops, assigned to Great Britain, there were a few hundred Indian soldiers being taken back from the Middle East to their homes in India, for a furlough. These Hindu soldiers and officers had been serving under the British military command in the Middle East. India was still a British Dominion, even though Mahatma Ghandi had tried for many years to break his country away from the British Empire and gain independence. All these Indian soldiers resented deeply having to serve in the British Army against their will, and they did not hide their hatred for the British.

The journey from the port of Basra to Bombay lasted several days. The Indian Ocean is known for being constantly rough and stormy. During that spring the "rough ocean" was particularly mean, and our little ship was tossed up and down by angry sea demons like a little toy box. That was my first voyage on any sea. It didn't seem to make such a tremendous impression on me; that is, I took the roughness in stride. I was still making up for my years of starvation, and I devoured the meals served on the ship with great enthusiasm. Sometimes I even supplemented my own meals with the dinners of other people, who were always on the verge of vomiting, even though they had not had food for days. The Indians were especially susceptible to sea-sickness. Most of them spent their time running around in search of an open porthole, then sticking their heads out through the holes and emptying their guts to feed the sea creatures. They looked very unhappy throughout the entire voyage to Bombay.

We were told during that passage that German and Japanese submarines were cruising the Indian and Atlantic oceans, hunting for ships flying the flag of any members of the Western Alliance—Great Britain, France, Norway, the United States, and other countries. Several Allied ships, merchant as well as warships, had been sunk in the Indian Ocean.

We arrived safely in the port of Bombay, perhaps because the navigator had orders to keep the ship as close to the coastline as safety considerations permitted.

Bombay was a huge, dirty port-city, teeming with thousands of poor people, child beggars, pavement sleepers, and sprawling urban slums. It is unforgettable. Amongst the sea of noisy bazaars, streets are tangled with impassable traffic, fashionable high-rise apartment buildings, and skyscrapers. There are also the very rich merchants and industrialists. All these people can be seen mixed together in the traditional annual religious ceremonies by the ocean shores. Above all these unbelievable crowds in this most cosmopolitan of India's cities stands the magnificent Taj Mahal, built in the seventeenth century. We were all tremendously impressed by the whole city, particularly by the very conspicuous Taj Mahal. We were en route to Great Britain, so our limited stay did not allow us much time for sightseeing. However, a couple of days after being placed in a camp near Deolali, a small town adjoining the city, we got passes to visit the city's wonders.

We toured the city in a group. For fun and entertainment we tried getting rides in a riksha. We also managed to visit the Kamatipura district, the red-light district of Bombay. Brothels are legal in Bombay, partly because the Hindu and Moslem religions are tolerant towards this kind of institution, and also because of the constant imbalance between males and females in the city. Some of our boys did avail themselves of the services of the local young beauties, but I apparently was not sufficiently physically recovered as yet, because I did not feel the urge for these encounters. I could only look and admire the young attractive girls who were my age, or even younger. The Soviet guard in the Lutsk prison, Commissar Kapusta, had predicted correctly when he prophesied that "we may survive, but we would not feel like enjoying ourselves."

Now we were waiting in Bombay for a ship to come and take us on the next leg of our journey, *i.e.*, to Great Britain. In about six weeks, a huge American merchant ship, drafted into military service, arrived in Bombay. We were ordered to get ready for embarkation. This ship was called *Mary Posa*. The military intelligence sources notified our command that the Indian Ocean was relatively calm and free of the enemy (Axis) submarines.

In a couple of days after getting the orders, we were

again transported by military personnel trucks back to the harbor, where the *Mary Posa* was waiting for us. This transport ship was huge in comparison to the steamer that had brought us from Basra in Persia to Bombay. About two thousand troops were loaded onto the *Mary Posa*, and we set off in the direction of the Cape of Good Hope in South Africa. Our sea route led by way of Madagascar, apparently so as not to be exposed unnecessarily to the enemy submarines.

Our journey westward across the Indian Ocean was rather uneventful, except for the whispered news being passed around among our troops that enemy subs had been detected by the Allied reconnaissance planes lurking in certain parts of the ocean. The *Mary Posa* was fast enough to evade the enemy subs because it could develop speeds far above the capabilities of the subs. The waters of the Indian Ocean were also constantly patrolled by the Alllied warships and planes.

As we approached Table Bay, with its interesting silhouette of Table Mountain, we felt pleasant relief at having accomplished successfully another very dangerous part of our journey. The climate of the Cape of Good Hope greeted us with beautiful, sunny weather. We were also received well by the friendly port authorities, since our ship was flying the United States flag. When we docked in the port of Capetown, we immediately experienced the feeling of being in friendly hands. We were not totally disembarking, but we got passes for visiting the charming Capetown and were advised to go out in twos or threes to avoid getting into any risky or dangerous encounters. From the point of view of meeting the local people, we were apparently in no danger. South Africa was then a part of the British Commonwealth, and our Royal Air Force badges and shoulder patches saying *Poland* assured for us a friendly introduction everywhere. Like in every port city in the world, there were many places of entertainment, and friendly folks to show us around the many charming and beautiful places where we could enjoy the lighter side of life. The young people, our friendly guides, were descendants of marriages between the British, the Dutch, and the Boers, who now proudly called themselves Afrikaners. The girls of that descent were particularly attractive and good looking. They had charming, exotic fragrances about them. They welcomed us almost like war heroes, because the official government propaganda news broadcasts gave plenty of attention to the war against Nazi Germany.

In our sightseeing tours around the area we were struck by many contradictions and paradoxes. In a country that openly prided itself on democratic principles and a democratically elected government we noticed that democracy there applied only to the white Afrikaners. The black natives, born and raised there, were for the most part left out of the democratic systems and processes. The blacks were not permitted to mix socially with whites at all, since most of South Africa's political institutions and laws were designed to serve only the white constituency. Now, in 1988, thirty-five years later, the situation has improved some, yet equality is still beyond the horizon.

18
Great Britain—Service in the Allied Air Force

Our stay in Capetown was extended by a couple of weeks because the intelligence reports indicated that the Atlantic Ocean had plenty of both German and Japanese enemy submarines prowling around. Another transport of troops from the Middle East, which had left Capetown about a month before we were due to set sails, was sunk by a sub just off the West African coast.

According to the military reports received, not many of the over two thousand military men that started out of Capetown were fished out of the stormy ocean waters. We were hoping that our *Mary Posa* would outwit the subs and deliver us safely to Great Britain.

The last part of our ocean voyage, Capetown to Scotland, took over two weeks. Our destination was Greenock, Scotland, just outside the great port of Glasgow on the River Clyde. Upon arrival in Scotland we breathed a deep sigh of relief and complete happiness. It felt extremely good to be at last on firm ground among the Allies. We were quickly disembarked amd taken directly to the railway station in Glasgow. The war was at its peak and no time was wasted for any formal greetings, speeches, or any emotionalism; all military movements had to be done secretly and under camouflage. At the railway station we were told that our next destination was the sea resort town of Blackpool, England. We were tired, but elated, nevertheless, at being so close to our final destination. This was an entirely new experience for us all; a new country, with a social order and habits altogether different from the ones we had ever been exposed to, and a new, strange language to learn. We were mostly aware of the general circumstances at the time; the war raged on in its most savage intensity. The German Luftwaffe bombers ruthlessly harassed and destroyed British cities day and night, sending millions of Britons out of the cities into the countryside in search of less threatened areas. The German Luftwaffe dumped tons of incendiary and destructive bombs upon the cities, especially the major metropolitan areas and industrial centers. The cities of London, Coventry, Manchester, Liverpool, and many others were reduced to ashes and ruins. Commercial buildings and factories were burning and collapsing daily. Hitler and his generals were determined to break the spirit of the British people and their Allies. Wartime leader Winston Churchill was heroically inspiring his people to keep watch constantly and put the fires out before they had a chance to spread too far.

The people of Blackpool were very hospitable to us. We were coming in as Allied soldiers, to lend our effort to the defense of their country. We were assigned to private apartments for temporary quarters, since there were many more military people in that small seaside resort than could fit in the available military barracks.

Myself and four other airmen were assigned to live in the apartment of Mr. and Mrs. Hubert Blake. From the first day of our stay at the Blakes' a feeling of warmth and friendship pervaded the household. It was the British type of friendship, slightly reserved, and yet genuinely appealing. The Blakes lived in a large, comfortable apartment facing the seaside, by the Irish Sea, on Promenade Avenue.

Mr. Hubert Blake was a machine operator. He worked long hours in a factory producing war-related products. His wife Eloise had worked in an office for some time before our arrival. Having their apartment in the midst of the vacation strip, they managed a lucrative part-time business of renting rooms to the vacationers. Since the vacation business was slack during the war, the Blakes had contracted with His Majesty's War Office to provide billeting, or living quarters for military personnel.

We were officially assigned to the Polish section of His Majesty's Royal Air Force (RAF). Soon we were equipped with the British guns, RAF's new blue uniforms with patches saying *Poland* on the shoulder strap.

Our first real problem was the complete inability to communicate in the English language. We were welcomed in all social circles, as Allies and as men, because of the acute scarcity of civilian men. Those men who were around in the city were fully occupied in the various aspects of the war effort, either in factories or in the military service. We, the newcomers from the Middle East, were allowed a few days of reprieve from most duties, to rest, eat, sleep, and do some sightseeing. New acquaintances were started; the girls were aplenty and anxious to teach us their language, customs, and to show us around.

Mrs. Blake, through a natural turn of events, soon became my English tutor. I had to repeat after her many times over and over again: "Good morning," "Good afternoon," or "Good night, Mrs. Blake," "Yes, please," or "No, thank you," or "Hello, how are you?" and so on. Mrs. Blake was most patient with me and after several lessons she said I was a good student. In a few days I learned to say several basic expressions, and it pleased my tutor.

I spent more and more time with Mrs. Blake, learning the English tongue. Since Mr. Blake was absent from home a great deal, Mrs. Blake was left alone to run the business with the Air Force boys at home. It seemed as though she enjoyed doing much of that business with me. She started using me as her assistant to get certain messages and instructions through to the boys.

Mrs. Eloise Blake was about twenty-six years old when she greeted us at her house. She was medium height, with short brown hair that was always perfectly groomed. She was slightly overweight for her small stature, but the excess weight was very attractively distributed. Her almost-round face was rather plain looking, but very femininely attractive, with the nose slightly upturned, and happily smiling eyes. They had been married for some six years, but the marriage didn't appear to be of much importance to Mr. Blake. They had not been blessed with any offspring. My skills in English didn't stretch far enough for me to ask complex personal questions or why this or that had happened. Anyway, even if I did ask, I wasn't sophisticated enough to understand complex answers that she would have given to such questions.

Eloise invited me several times to go out with her during the day when she had a slow time between meals. She was, I thought, very patient as a teacher of English to me, and I was anxiously soaking it all up like a dried-up natural sponge. Soon I acquired an English-Polish dictionary and a notebook. In my spare time away from the tutoring sessions I labored writing out English words and their meanings in Polish. I wrote any and all words that I came across into the notebook, and then I searched for their Polish equivalents.

The boys began to come to me with letters they had received from their new girlfriends and asked me to get some meaning out of those letters, because they hadn't made much of a start in their effort to unscramble the mysteries of the English language. I had to dig through my dictionary, word by word, to translate their letters. That made me a little proud of my newly acquired lead among my friends and it served as an incentive to double up my efforts in studying English. With the help of my tutor and the English-Polish dictionary, I could begin to communicate with my dates. Still, I was amazed at how little knowledge of the common language was needed to nourish a lover's relationship. It seemed so, anyway.

In the hours on my own, I often roamed around the town. The North Pier Amusement Town, with its many game machines, flashing lights, electric trains for riding, electric cars with rubber bumpers, and hundreds of people, fascinated me. I was entranced, like Alice in Wonderland. All of that, and being able to go wherever I wished, even getting lost in a blind alley. That was fun, too, because then I had a chance to pull out my stock list of phrases and ask people for directions to get back to the Promenade.

Unrestricted freedom! What deep, delightful satisfaction, even happiness can one experience from simply being able to walk out into the street in a strange city. Nobody, not even a guard, followed me around. I could even miss meals sometimes, and still Eloise greeted me with a smile. She would just say, "Richard, naughty, naughty!"

I had to ask her how that new word was spelled so I could look it up in my dictionary. When I found out the meaning of that word, my cheeks blushed and I said, "I am verry, verry sorry, Mrs. Blake."

One day Mr. Hubert Blake took me to a pub. There,

I was further amazed at seeing the contented, carefree life of the pub, throbbing with its own loud pulse. I could see no war weariness in there. There were barrels of beer, laughter, masculine wild stories of fishing, hunting, or some romantic conquests being told, where the close-knit audience responded with great appreciation. There was no sign anywhere that no women were admitted, but there were no women in the pub. It was a tradition that only men were to come into the pub.

There was a lot of singing every day, accounts of football (soccer) games, individual foolery, and hearty laughter. For me, it was another occasion to expand my command of the English language. I brought home with me at least a pageful of new words.

One Friday afternoon Eloise unexpectedly said to me, "Richard, do you know how to dance?"

It made me think with nostalgia of the times when my sister and her girlfriends taught me to dance. That seemed so far in the past—it was worlds away from my present environment. I wondered if the type of dancing I had learned under the thatched roof of my Uncle John's home would be suitable for a ballroom in Blackpool, England. I answered rather uncertainly, "My sister teach me dance, but I know not if I can dance here."

"All right, Richard. We will go to a dance tonight, you and I," she answered, quite cheerfully.

That meant that I had a date for the evening. By 8:00 P.M., when the last traces of the dinner mess were cleaned up, Eloise went upstairs to her room. She came back down shortly, totally transformed. She had on a trim, modest, but outstandingly elegant dress and looked smashingly attractive, as the Lancashire people would say.

I wore my air force uniform. Inwardly, I was elated and somewhat proud of myself. This was going to be a very different experience for me. A new world was perhaps opening up for me.

We took a tram car down the Promenade to the Winter Gardens. We saw thousands of people having fun with a variety of games and amusements on the pier. We made our way to the ballroom. At the entrance, Eloise paid for both our tickets, which she told me about ahead of time, so I wouldn't feel embarrassed. She knew that Airman Class 1 pay wasn't very generous. There were a few hundred couples already there, and the music had started.

I was greatly impressed by the splendor of the ballroom, the lighting effects, and the huge dance floor. On both sides of the ballroom floor there were a number of easy chairs and settees, lavishly furnished in plush maroon. I was ready to stand and stare around in wonderment, but Eloise nudged me and said, "Let's go inside and sit down."

My admiring staring around at all this lavish wonderland was only interrupted, but it wasn't stopped. We went inside, downstairs, where the entrance to the dance floor was. My partner was anxious to start dancing. The six- or seven-member band was playing the slow waltz. In Lutsk, my sister and her girlfriends had called it the English waltz, and I had a lot of practice in dancing it. One of my sister's girlfriends, Halina Krasinska, a beautiful blond about three years older than I, whom I idolized, used to like dancing the English waltz with me. But we always had such a skimpy little piece of hard-mud floor for dancing in my Uncle John's thatch-roofed house that there was hardly enough space in which to fully develop the rich, ambling strides and the gracious, circular rhythm of the waltz.

Now, after first finding my poise and testing the slipperiness of the beautiful parquet floor, I rediscovered my long-dormant talent for dancing. I loved it. I was fascinated, as if I were in another world. Some dark memories (from the other world) kept gnawing at my subconsciousness, but I couldn't let them stir me out of this wonderful spell—I just danced and danced.

Eloise may have been a little heavier than I, but on the dance floor she seemed almost weightless. I was aware of her being with me, yet we became as one, and I just felt her happy face next to mine and her smiling eyes that expressed deep approval. Her body pulsated with released energy, in complete abandon. We didn't want to stop until exhaustion caught up with us. We made wide circles and loops on the spacious floor, easily finding our path among scores of dancing couples.

After a brief intermission, the band changed the pace for the next dance and I had to try my skill on a foxtrot. That also went well, though not quite as well as the slow waltz, which was my favorite. Then came tangos, fast waltzes, and more foxtrots. Eloise wanted to dance two dances quite new to me, the quickstep and the Lambeth walk, both of which I had never done before. At first I hesitated, as I was not sure of my ability to do it correctly, and I did not want to subject my charming partner to ridicule. But she insisted that we would do well, and I played the role of a gentleman and submitted to her wish. Her faith in my dancing talent prodded me to do my very best. The Lambeth walk proved to be "a piece of cake," as the Britons say, and it was a lot of fun!

Eloise was a very talented dancer. She managed to lead me so tactfully that I didn't even realize I was being led—I dared to think I was a good dancer.

Thus my newly acquired rhythms, the quickstep and the Lambeth walk were fun, and I thanked Eloise for introducing me to them. We danced all evening, taking breaks only when the band took their rest.

The whole evening was a success. Eloise was satisfied, judging by the expression of her eyes. On the way home, before we got on the tram, we stopped by a fish-and-chips stand and Eloise ordered two servings of fish and chips. Both were served to us extra fresh and steaming hot, in a newspaper.

Apparently there were many shortages in the country, caused by the war conditions, and one of them was a lack of paper of any kind. Any available supply of paper went through several uses before it was disposed of for recycling. England imported almost all of its paper products, and in war time such goods were not very high on the list of essential priorities.

When we boarded the home-bound tram car, I saw that that was the custom at the time. Most passengers were eating fish and chips from a newspaper, smacking their lips and licking their fingers.

Eloise whispered in my ear, "Thank you, Richard, thank you. I had a smashing time."

I drew her close to me and answered, "I thank you, Eloise. I love dance with you." Then I said, "My sister dance me much."

At that stage of my English lessons I didn't know much about the past tense. But I was happy and pleased that Eloise had taken me out. I rediscovered myself as a social being and quickly gained confidence in that realm.

I had been surrounded by suffering and death for so long that I looked at the living world from the other side of the grave. So much was utterly irrelevant here that people took as important. It took a while for me to learn to judge the world from the live side of the grave, and Eloise helped a lot.

At home Eloise made some tea for us and we sat on the couch and listened to the radio music. She complained to me that Hubert liked to spend weekend nights late at the pub, and she felt lonely.

I was young, naive, and innocent. I was anxious, impatient, still full of personal fear, and socially inexperienced. Above all, I felt very insecure in this new environment. I sensed that what my dancing partner was about to do was not quite all right morally. She approached me, but she, too, soon realized that things were happening too quickly. She hugged and kissed me tenderly, and then said quickly, "Richard, I didn't realize it was so late; let's go to sleep." She ran toward her bedroom downstairs and indicated my bedroom upstairs.

I was excited and frustrated at the same time. I felt happy and elated that such a lovely lady was interested in me as a man and as a social being—I didn't know how to respond or what to do. In my mind, visions flashed back . . . the three women whom I loved dearly—my mother, my aunt Frances, and sister Maria. How could I make myself worthy of their approval again? Then I saw Commissar Kapusta shouting that we would not feel like enjoying ourselves.

I knew then that Commissar Kapusta's prediction (or curse?) held no more power over me. It felt so wonderful to be a young and healthy man, to be wanted, and to be free!

Epilogue

After the events told in this book, I served in the Allied Air Force, in the RAF units, for more than four years, at first as a radio operator, later as an instructor and interpreter in the air force radio school.

Toward the end of the World War II, when there was no more need to train additional radio operators, I tried to enroll in the civilian radio mechanics' school, but I was not accepted. Priorities for acceptance to those civilian trade schools were given to British citizens. I then turned my attention to general education. I applied and was accepted to the Polish *gimnazjum* (high school) and *Lyceum* (junior college). In three years I was matriculated from the Polish Business Lyceum, and shortly afterwards I won, through a competitive examination, acceptance and a tuition scholarship to Ohio University in Athens.

After several months of negotiations with several American and British officials and a great deal of patience, I finally arrived at LaGuardia Airport in New York City. It was January 1949. During the customs interview at LaGuardia by an officer of the Immigration and Naturalization Service, I had to declare my financial condition. I owned and had on me a total of ninety-three dollars. When the Immigration and Naturalization Service agent heard that my total assets amounted to ninety-three dollars, the officer immediately concluded that such an amount was woefully insufficient for a four-year program of studies at Ohio University. The officer ordered me put in the detention center (prison) at Ellis Island in the New York harbor. Thus I again found myself locked up behind prison bars, but this time I at least had a chance to admire, through the iron bars, the beautifully lit-up Statue of Liberty, holding her torch in the outstretched arm, inviting and welcoming the "huddled and oppressed" human masses. This ordeal lasted for seven days, until the whole misunderstanding was settled through the kindness of the interviewing officer, who arranged for a contact to be made with the Polish Immigration Committee in Brooklyn, New York. The late Father Burant, then the director of the Brooklyn post of the P.N.A. (Polish National Alliance), issued a security bond to the Immigration and Naturalization Service guaranteeing my return to Great Britain on the completion of my studies at Ohio University, unless another type of visa could be obtained.

After spending seven days in the Ellis Island detention center and answering all questions given me by the immigration agents satisfactorily, I obtained formal permission to proceed on to Ohio University.

Four years at the University of Ohio went by awfully fast. I had almost no spare time between studying and working here and there, mostly with private employers, because I had no official permit to be gainfully employed. My four-year efforts were awarded by the diploma I received—B.Sc. (Comm.) in Business Administration. Even before graduation day, a representative of Montgomery Ward and Company, canvassing the graduating students at Ohio University, offered employment to me as a business correspondent in the Credit and Collection department. With the B.Sc. diploma and a firm job offer, and not much else, I arrived at Montgomery Ward's main corporate office in Chicago.

It turned out that the offer I received at Athens, Ohio, was not honored by the manager of the personnel department. This discrepancy led me to lose trust in that company's policy toward its employees.

Within two months' time after taking the job at the Montgomery Ward & Company, I found an accountant's job at Standard Oil Company (Ind.). It was difficult to find an apartment in those postwar years, so I had to sublet a small sleeping-room temporarily, until a full-size apartment could be located. Thus I felt myself to have established the economic base for starting a family. Next I wrote to a Scottish lass in Glasgow, Scotland, whom I had befriended while living there, and proposed marriage.

Mary accepted my offer quite willingly, and after completing the necessary official paperwork, Mary arrived in Chicago around Christmas in 1952. In the fall of 1953, Mary and I tied the matrimonial knot. A year later our first daughter was born, and in the following four years another daughter and two sons enriched our life. By that time we had bought our first house, sold it, and bought another one, all in the northwestern section of the city of Chicago.

My ambition was to obtain a master's degree. I set off toward this goal in 1955 and succeeded by the summer of 1960 at DePaul University in Chicago, Illinois.

Throughout the 1960s, there were three waves of layoffs at Standard Oil Company (Indiana), and I, along with thousands of clerical employees, finally got the corporate ax in 1968. I went back to college, to gain another major qualification, this time in education. The first three years of my teaching career, I taught high-school business subjects and English language, on a provisional teacher certificate. From then on until the present, I have given my full time and attention to teaching, mostly the English language and literature in English, although at times I have taught Polish and Russian, too. After working as a teacher for five years, I decided to gain more knowledge of the principles of education in the U.S. I enrolled in a public policy analysis program at the University of Illinois, at the Chicago Circle, which I completed in 1981. I then was granted a Ph.D. (Ed.) degree.

Appendix: Russia's Drive for Domination

> *Where the Russian flag had once been hoisted, it must never be lowered.*
> —Tsar Nicolas I (1854)
>
> *We are no pacifists. We are not in favor of peace at any price.*
> —Leonid Brezhnev (1978)
>
> *In October 1917 we parted with the Old World, rejecting it once and for all. We are moving toward a new world, the world of Communism. We shall never turn off that road.*
> —Mikhail Gorbachev (November 2, 1987)

Russia's expansionistic tendencies are not a new phenomenon. They started over four hundred years ago, when Tsar Ivan, called by the historians "the Terrible," (1533–84), finally conquered the Khanate of Kazan. Ivan the Terrible used techniques that present rulers in the Kremlin apply so well, over and over again—undercover agents, discontented subjects, and bribed members of the state they wish to conquer. For more than thirty years, the tsar's agents worked like social termites among the Khan's subjects, to provoke and artificially sustain domestic unrest, and to demoralize and corrupt the nation.

The conquests by Soviet Russia, during and since World War II, of many European countries, e.g., Poland, Romania, Estonia, Latvia, Lithuania, Hungary, Yugoslavia, Albania, East Germany, Czechoslovakia, Bulgaria, and countries in other parts of the world—North Korea, the Kurile and Sakhalin Islands, North Vietnam, and the

146 / The First Polish Republic (1569-1795)

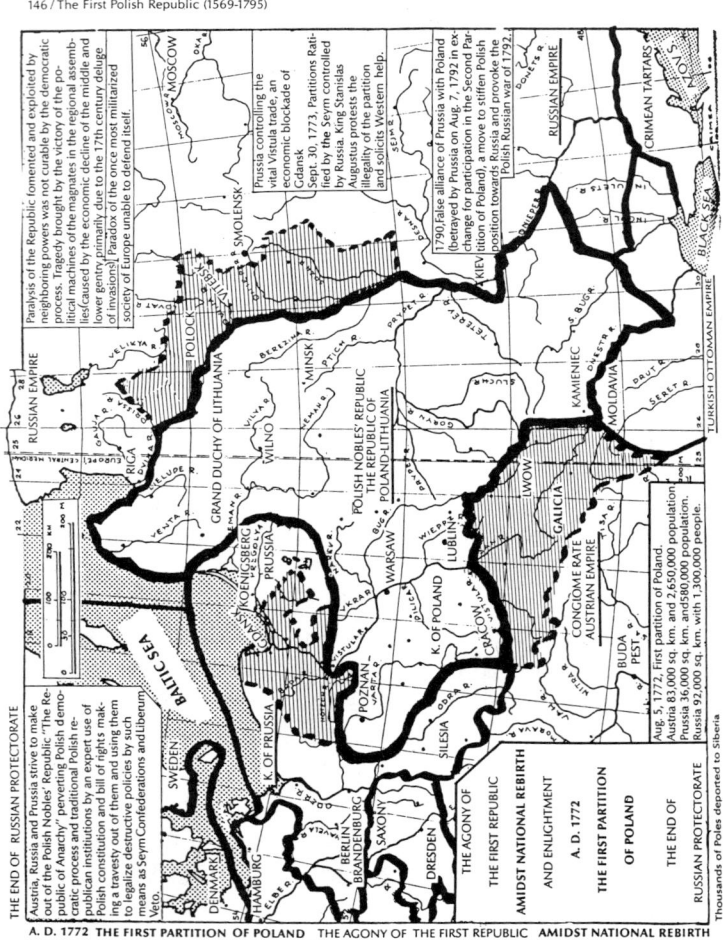

A.D. 1772 THE FIRST PARTITION OF POLAND THE AGONY OF THE FIRST REPUBLIC AMIDST NATIONAL REBIRTH
Map: 1772 The First Partition of Poland During National Rebirth.

From Poland: *A Historical Atlas* by Iwo Pogonowski, published by Hippocrene Books, Inc., 171 Madison Ave., New York, NY 10016, p. 146.

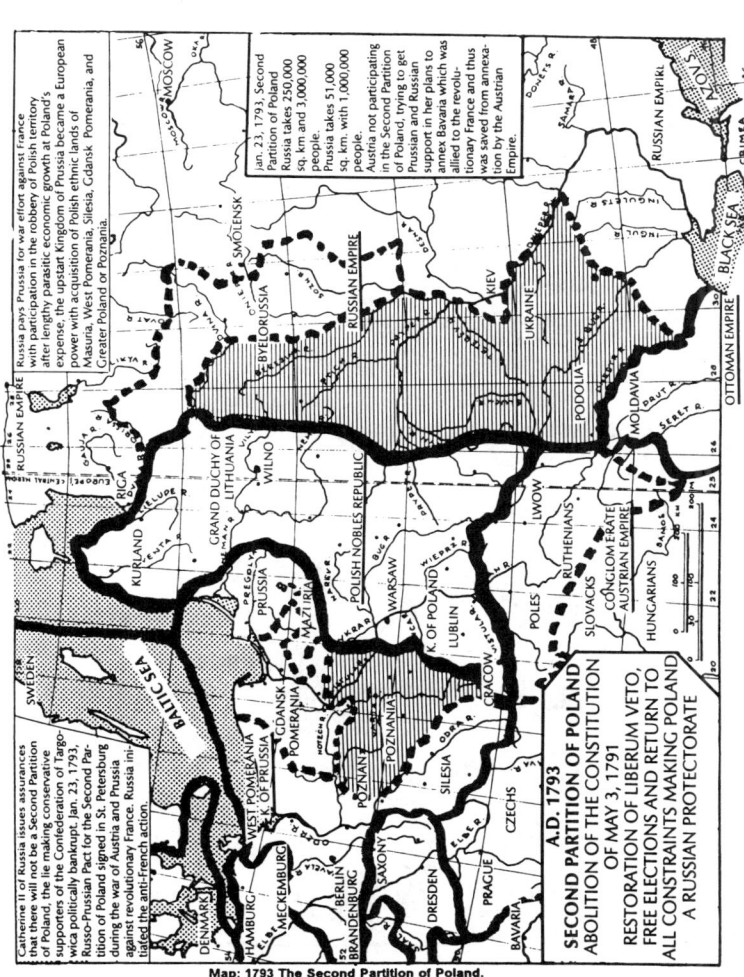

From Poland: A Historical Atlas, *p. 149.*

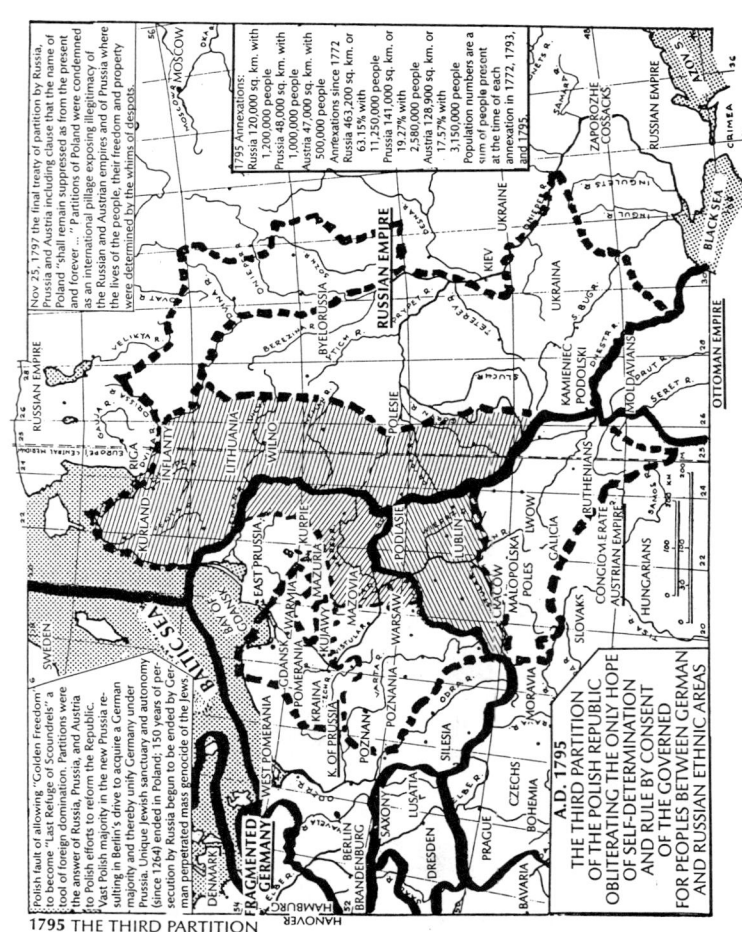

From *Poland: A Historical Atlas, p. 151.*

Map: 1795 The Third Partition of Poland.

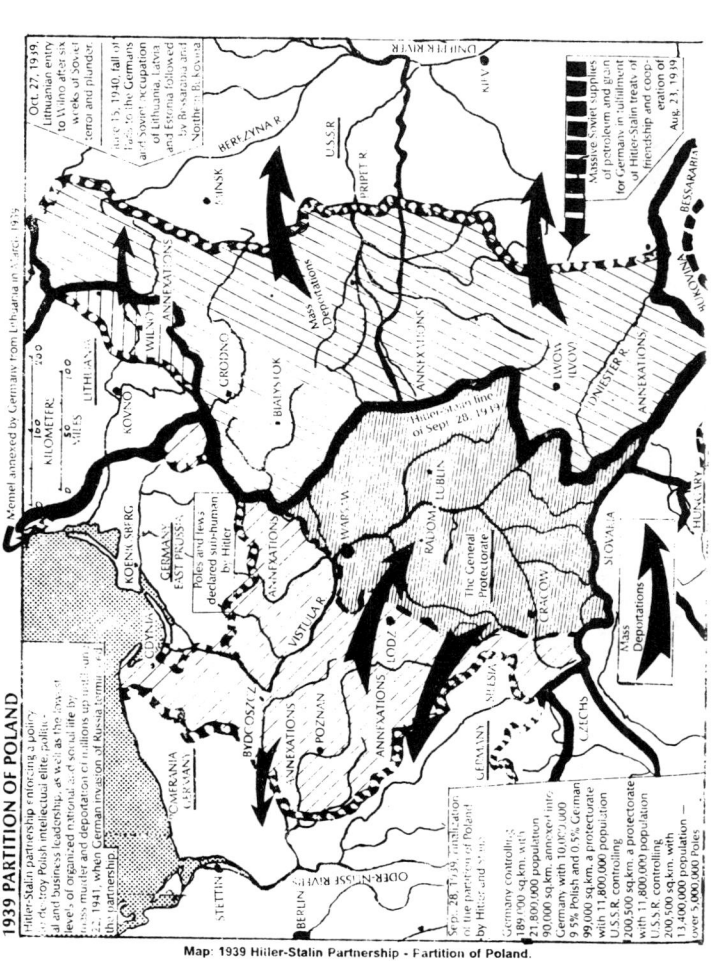

Map: 1939 Hitler-Stalin Partnership - Partition of Poland.

From Poland: A Historical Atlas, p. 200.

© 1980 by National Review, Inc., 150 East 35th Street, New York, NY

MOSCOW'S OUTWARD THRUST
"We are no pacifists. We are not in favor of peace at any price."
Leonid Brezhnev

0016. Reprinted with permission.

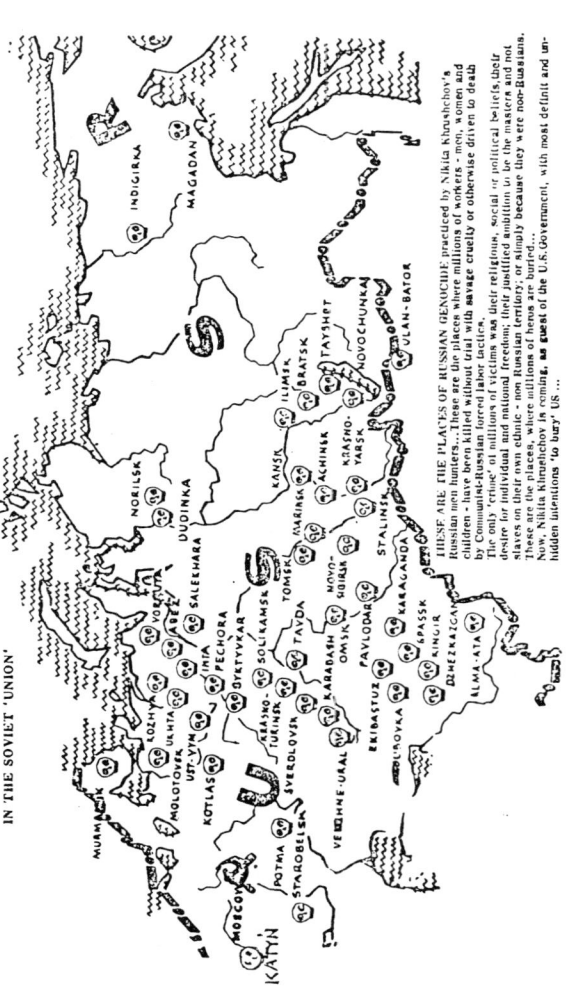

Source unknown; see copyright page.

most recent, Afghanistan—are just examples of their relentless expansion outward. The Soviets have learned their lessons from Ivan the Terrible exceptionally well.

The twentieth-century territorial gains achieved by communist Russia have all followed exactly the methods developed and practiced by Tsar Ivan.

A very scholarly work was done by the late Jan V. Nanaushvili* explains these methods and the results of their application.

He was a native of the Republic of Georgia, which has been ruled by the Kremlin since 1921. The book contains a wealth of information on the methods used by the successive masters of Russian imperialism.

Most western politicians, misled by Russian dissidents, including Solzhenitzyn, and their followers, the common folks, have been blaming not Russia, but communists, for the brutal and deceitful ways of Soviet conquests since the 1917 Revolution. Not so Mr. Nanaushvili—he saw no great change in the direction of Russian political thinking, nor in their methods of dealing with the people, inside or outside of Russia.

About the year 1480, the Muscovite Princedom freed itself from the shackles of Mongolian enslavement, which had dominated it for 240 years. Very soon, the Muscovites launched their aggressive hordes outward, to conquer surrounding Mongolian nations. They became even more efficient than the Mongolians at enslaving other people. The Mongolians were known for their tolerance of the subjugated people's religious and social ways. The Russians since Ivan the Terrible have always insisted on totally converting the people they conquered, not only in matters of

*Jan Nanuashvili, *What Everyone in the Free World Should Know about Russia* (New York: Vantage Press, Inc., 1973).

religion, but also language, social, political, and ideological systems.

Russian policy has not changed much over the last four hundred years. Its main characteristics have been: 1) the aim to dominate the world; 2) the moral corruption of its consecutively isolated victims, destruction of their state, and the final conquest by means of peaceful aggression or by military coup; and 3) the limiting of all facets of internal life, forcibly lowering the level of existence to that of a war apparatus faced with an enemy, until their vision of liberation is in place.

The successive rulers of Russia have learned these rules very well, which the evidence shows:
• Russia has been victorious in all local conquests within a short period of time, usually no longer than a couple of decades at most. None of the subjugated nations has ever managed to free itself from the Russian bear's grip. (Poland's liberation from the tsarist occupation in 1918 and successful defense of its independence in 1920 was a temporary exception—because in 1939, Poland again succumbed to the overwhelming power and diabolic cunningness of the Russians. It must be noted that when Poland fell, so did all the neighboring states, Lithuania, Latvia, Estonia, Romania, Hungary and Czechoslovakia.)
• Russia has now cleared its path of aggression in all directions: the Pacific, the Indian Ocean, the Mediterranean, and the Atlantic.
• Russia has now reached the stage of direct preparation for the war of domination of the world under the camouflage of communism. This war could proceed, consistently toppling governments in succession, until the conquest is complete.

The drama of the Polish nation, which the Russians have tried to subjugate and "Russify" ever since the middle of the eighteenth century, was briefly (for twenty years) interrupted between the two world wars (1918–1939). Then, in 1945, Joseph Stalin's cold aggressiveness and unyielding demands shrewdly forced Mr. Churchill and Franklin D. Roosevelt to consent to the Russian "extension of their sphere of influence." This action was a political and ideological letdown, bordering on treason, by Poland's Western Allies (Great Britain and the U.S.). These two Western Allies should have known that by "sphere of influence" the Russians meant complete political and economic occupation. When the three wartime leaders, Churchill, Roosevelt, and Stalin, met in February, 1945 at Yalta, in southern Russia, they agreed that free elections would be held in Poland and other Eastern European countries. The meeting at Yalta seemed to be a friendly one. But Stalin willed otherwise. He invited, in the spring of 1945, all national leaders from each of the countries in Russia's sphere of influence to come to a summit meeting in Moscow. After the meeting, all those who opposed Stalin's will to rule their countries were arrested, jailed, and later destroyed. Then the Russians went ahead and established puppet governments in each of those countries.

A few months later, in July 1945, after Truman succeeded FDR as president, the three leaders met again, at Potsdam. When Truman questioned Stalin about all pro-Soviet governments in Eastern European countries and demanded immediate free elections in accordance with the Yalta agreement, Stalin refused. Stalin stated, "A freely elected government in any of these Eastern European countries would be anti-Soviet, and that we cannot allow." There was no further reaction on that subject from the two western partners at the Yalta conference.

Since then, all Eastern European countries have again been shackled by brutal Russian colonization. The Russian conquests are invariably accompanied by cruel barbarism towards the conquered people. Their main and ultimate goal is to russify the people. Certain local tribes in Siberia have been totally destroyed, others completely russified. The Russians have always attempted to explain and to justify their conquests with some ideological motives—in the East it was the need to bring culture to the Asians; in the West it was to defend their orthodox Christian religion and panslavism. From the time of the Bolshevik Revolution in 1917, it was to bring worldwide internationalism and communism (under Russian management!).

The Russians do not believe in any other brand of communism. It has to be Russian communism. Conversion of China to communism was not enough. The continued clashes of Russia and China along their common borders offers proof that no brand of communism independent of Russian domination will be tolerated by the Russian bosses. After the Russians conquer a country or region, with the help of the local communists, one of the first things they do is to incarcerate all the local communist activists. Or they may send them to the labor camps for an extensive (usually ten years) "retraining course." It seldom happens that these retrained former ethnic "prophets of utopia" get out alive from their school of new communism. In either case, they seldom return to their native country.

It is significant that the thirst for conquests and imperialism invariably exist in the Russian mentality. It is not cancelled out by even the most real differences of the political or social biases or preferences among the various Russian peoples. Russian literature has served the tsarist imperialism well, and so it does now. In the framework of this patriotic service to the Fatherland, geniuses such as Pushkin, Lermontov, Dostoyevsky, and others created masterpieces that glorified the territorial accomplishments of their leaders of the past.

The present-day Russian patriots, so-called dissidents, avowed enemies of the present political system, are not free from the same imperialistic mentality. One of them, Amalric, says, ". . . The Ukrainians and Lithuanians I suppose could exist within the framework of the Soviet Union. . . . "

It appears from this kind of statement that only Russians have the right to enjoy independence and to be classified as a power, but neither the Ukrainians, Lithuanians, nor any other ethnic group should be entitled to such rights. Their fate should be to exist within the framework of the Soviet Union, i.e., Russia. Similar political ideas prevail among the so-called "white" Russian intelligentsia in the west, who are openly in opposition to the present "red" Russian tsarism. That was a major problem in 1920, during the Bolshevik invasion into Poland, when the white (tsarist) Russian government could not come to any agreement with the newly established Polish government. The new Polish leaders were anxious to enter into a cooperative action with the tsarist Russian leaders, then struggling with their revolutionary Russian brothers. The Russian generals demanded, however, in exchange for such cooperation, that the Poles hold in trust for Russia the formerly Polish eastern territories, until then occupied by the tsarist Russia for 123 years—and transfer those lands back to the tsarist government when the fighting was finished, if that government should survive. In other words, the white Russians insisted on ". . . one and indivisible Russia." The Polish leaders, including the Polish Marshal and the head of the state government, J. Pilsudski, then decided to fight alone against the Bolsheviks. Then the Romanov dynasty, which ruled Russia for more than three hundred years (1613–1917), ceased to exist.

Conquests in Russian plans must inevitably end in the russification of the conquered nation—there is no other alternative. Only the time set for this process may be different for each victimized nation. It can be said with certainty that whatever slogans or principles are proclaimed for the justification of the conquests, these slogans oblige only the people being conquered; the Russians themselves do not have to be concerned about these principles.

The catchwords, slogans or battle cries are for export, to the people whose land and homes have been annexed or conquered. From the Russian point of view, the slogans have to lead them to the same Matushka Rossiya (Mother Russia).

Russian conquests are solidified by means of the police muzzle of a totalitarian system. Without such a system, such as through an "open" society, they would not be able to attain their ends. This brings Russia to the old vicious circle: The totalitarian system furthers aggression in order to justify its existence, and the conquered territories require a totalitarian police system, red or white, in order to avoid disintegration. This circle is the only *modus vivendi* for Russia. Representatives of all Russian political shades are well aware of this fact. Without the police system to hold the totalitarian state in place, disintegration is inevitable. Much of the dissatisfaction of the people in Russia and in nations subjugated by Russia is due to the economic and day-to-day strains that maintenance of a totalitarian system causes. It requires many, many resources to maintain such a war machine. Countries around the world experience the drain on resources that maintenance of a large military strength puts on the common man. Individuals are ultimately the ones who suffer most from buildups of military power. The strongest experience of this drain on resources is in a totalitarian police state.

The Russian people, throughout centuries of national existence, have never known a true democracy. For a short period, a type of democracy lasted, but only seven months and twenty-five days, from February 27 to October 25, 1917, between the fall of the tsarist absolute rule and the Bolshevik counterrevolution. That was the period of Kerensky's government, which was organized on democratic principles, but the leaders of the mass of the people in revolt opted for the centrally controlled, totalitarian system.

The political police system, on which totalitarian rule is based, was created by Ivan the Terrible in about 1565. It has existed continuously under such names as Oprichina, Okhrana, Gendarmerie, Cheka, GPU, NKVD, MWD, and the present KGB. The Polish arm of this police system is now called Sluzba Bezpieczeństwa (Service of Social Safety), in short "S.B.," and the reins for its total control are held exclusively in the Kremlin.

During the reign of Tsar Peter the Great, and also during the time of Empress Catherine II, Russian agents had penetrated certain prominent Polish families among the top layer of the Polish nobility, the magnates, (Rzewuski, Branicki, Potocki, and a few others). The Russians made deals with various magnates, who, with generous support from the Kremlin, agreed to foster unrest and discontent among the nobility. They also planted the seeds of dissension and rebellion against the central government of the king and the Seym (Parliament). These treacherous magnates did their best to satisfy their foreign masters. In the middle half of the eighteenth century they were instrumental in enacting the law of Liberum Veto, which gave the power to any member of the Seym to prevent law and social order from being reestablished in Poland. From the reign of the first Saxon (elective) king, Augustus the Second (1697–1733), until 1795, three neighbors—Prussia, Russia, and Austria—did their corruptive work in Poland. Undercover efforts by Russian tsars in partnership with the Prussians, which lasted eighty years, finally demoralized and corrupted the Polish ruling class. This brought about the three partitions (1772, 1793, and 1795) and the final disappearance of the Polish state, for the next 123 years.

The essential ideology and methods used in the eighteenth century were not much different from the method used by Tsar Ivan the Terrible against the Khanate of Astrachan in the sixteenth century. Again, similarly staged techniques were deployed in the twentieth century, during and after WWII against the European countries of Estonia, Latvia, Lithuania, Rumania, Poland, and the Balkan states. One by one, the agents of the modern tsars, in service of the communist NKVD and the Commintern (Communist International) had spearheaded discontent and unrest in those countries, until native groups of malcontents and actual NKVD-supported agents were ready to welcome with flowers their Russian (this time, communist) masters.

Here are two examples of the present techniques for such termite destruction from the inside:

1. The fifth column, a network of espionage groups working in the target country, whose assignments are varied, including the gathering of information on military and industrial projects and channeling it to appropriate agents in the sending government, stirring unrest among people, and also organizing diversionary and espionage activities; and
2. The war of nerves, or neither war nor peace, or

any other term to camouflage the real perpetrators of constant state of tension and hostility without armed conflict. It may also include the organizing of local sabotage groups under the guise of workers' unions, whose aims are to foment social unrest and class war, without actually trying to bring about the betterment of the workers.

In the U.S., this technique uses certain minority groups, including black Americans, not financed directly by the Russians, but by their henchmen. An example is the case of the El Rukn, a black nationalist organization based in Chicago, that received support money from Russia, via Kadaffi's Libyan government. The foreign power provides the plan and the money. The plan has nothing officially to do with communism, because communism is a dirty word. El Rukn's assignment was to commit certain acts of terrorism by bombing specified objects in the U.S. This was being done not overtly as a communist organization, but under a religious-racial coverup, with which Russia was not even remotely officially connected. They were discovered in time and several members of the El Rukn organization were tried, convicted, and sentenced to prison terms. Many similar activities are engaged in by members of various minority groups, such as new arrivals in the U.S. among Hispanic, Polish, and other immigrant groups. They are "hooked" for these services with a promise of a better treatment for their families in the home country or by a threat of reprisals if they refuse. They frequently operate for years undiscovered. The consulates of countries of the Soviet bloc are known for carrying on recruiting and spying activities using temporary residents, who come to the U.S. for extended visits with their relatives. The results are the same social unrest and discontent, and a yearning for resolution by a "friend" from outside of one's own homeland.

Western countries are proclaiming the fight against communism as a sociopolitical dogma, and are making many peace deals with the Russians. The communist parties organized by Russian agents in most western countries are engaging these powers in small, relatively meaningless social skirmishes. In some countries local parties are organized for entirely legitimate purposes, such as to help alleviate a specially picked, socially disadvantaged group. The Russians use such organizations as nuclei, which in time get blown out of proportion by skillfully trained activists who build them up. In most cases they use professional groups, such as university professors, politicians, and journalists. In these kinds of places the Russians gain ground and establish crucially important strategic bases in new territories, such as Cuba, Angola, Ethiopia, Afghanistan, and Nicaragua.

Western countries dare not put up a determined front against Russian aggression, because the latter have skillfully managed to change enough minds of not only leftists, but also many trusting liberals. The result is that many "peaceniks" naively play into the Russian hands.

A characteristic form of summit negotiations between the U.S. and the Soviet Union was the agreement reached recently (December 1987). During the preliminary talks American politicians insisted on several demands, such as recognition of civil rights for the many Russian ethnic minorities and captive nations (see list in the back). This would include letting out of Russia those who want to leave, and that the Russians get their troops out of Afghanistan. The Russians said little or nothing in answer to those preliminary demands. When the time came close to the signing of the agreement, Mr. Gorbachev used all his charm and arrogance, alternatively, in his political interviews and said that, ". . . The United States has their own set of social problems, and the Soviet Union has its, and . . . let each country take care of its own problems." With regard to the Russian invasion of Afghanistan and the Russian troops murdering and maiming hundreds of thousands of the defenseless civilian population, Mr. Gorbachev said with a smile, as if he wasn't much concerned about this problem, ". . . We will get out of Afghanistan . . ," but he didn't say when. There were no objections and no more questions from the interviewers or from the audience. The agreement was later signed, nevertheless.

The fight continues on the home front, with civil-war barricades in the streets of Western nations (e.g., Honduras, Haiti, Nicaragua), while Western politicians are engaged in pursuing various disarmament agreements with the Russians. I hope future negotiators will be cautious and wise to include every possible precaution in drafting the text of the agreements with the Russians—and then make adequate allowance in their expectations of long-lasting benefits for both sides of the negotiating nations. The Russians, in the past, have honored many agreements only for as long as it suited them. They have violated all types of agreements, disarmament, nonagression, and coexistence as soon as the circumstances favored another action.

Most Americans are not aware that the last sixty treaties with the Russians have been broken. Few of the violations received much, if any, attention from the U.S. and world media.

How do the Russians achieve such an absolute, almost foolproof control over the souls of their victims in the newly conquered nations?

The patterns followed today with unbelievable success have been tried and perfected for more than four hundred years. For several centuries now, the Russian common people, including more than 100 million of their enslaved neighboring nations, have lived in constant terror of the "Big Brother" watching them. The all-pervasive spying network has been developed to perfection by the state secret police (the KGB). The whole method has been well described, analyzed, and documented in a book written by Jan Tomasz Gross and Irena Grudzinska-Gross.*

The authors describe how a very fine network of private citizens is organized even before the actual military invasion. Personal data is accumulated on numerous prominent people in the country being targeted for an attack. When the initial preparations are completed, and the opportune time comes for a social revolution in the target country, the groups of local communist agents are activated. A great deal of time, effort, and money are expended for an advance propaganda social war. Racial (in the U.S.) and class hatred are taught like the Bible truth in a regular American Sunday school. Many people who suffered personal persecution, real or imagined, are won over to assist the invader in toppling over the tyrannical and social structure. Once the Russian military units, with their merciless guns, move into the victim-country, a campaign of public and private terror is let loose. Denunciations are publicly encouraged and rewarded. In such a system, anybody who has any grudge, justified or fictitious, against somebody else, has a chance to turn his personal enemy in to the secret police, who will take care

*Jan Tomasz Gross and Irena Grudzinska Gross, *W Czterdziestym Nas Matko na Sybir Wyslali* (In 1940 They Sent Us to Siberia, Mum) (London: Aneks, 1983).

of him right away. The accused disappears for a long time, usually forever.

Jan and Irena Gross selected 130 compositions written by school children, out of more than twenty-three hundred such personal stories and thirty-five essays of adults out of more than ten thousand reports and stories collected in the archives of the Hoover Institute at Stanford, California. These were from various Polish civilians and military personnel in World War II. The children and adults wrote these reports soon after they were freed (between 1942 and 1945) from the Russian prisons and labor and resettlement camps.

According to these compositions, the deportations were carried out using a uniform pattern. Units of the local militia usually awoke their victims in the early morning, sometime after midnight. The families were allowed very little time, maybe a half hour to an hour, for packing their life-long accumulations of belongings. Then they were terrorized by the soldiers with bayonet-tipped rifles and forcefully loaded onto trucks. The trucks drove them directly to railway stations, where freight trains were waiting with doors already open. The deportees usually spent several weeks in those trains, some of them freezing to death in winter months, or dying from terrible heat during summer transports. Food and water were always inadequate and administered intermittently. A hole in the floor in the middle of the train car served in place of all their toilet and sanitary needs. Men, women, children, old people, even infants and seriously ill people traveled together. None were exempt from deportation. Polish people represented the predominant majority among deportees. However, no ethnic group was spared and neither was any social or occupational group pardoned—30 percent of deported people were Jews, 18 percent Ukrainians and Belorussians, and 52 percent were Polish people. Peasants and workers made up about 30 percent of the people deported from Poland, but only 3 percent of them were workers.

The Hitler-Stalin partnership agreed on a planned extermination of the leaders of the Polish nation. The map in the reference section following the appendix details various shipments of Polish citizens to Russian camps and prisons.

Once the Red Army got into the Polish territory, major operations aimed at terrorizing the whole population got under way. The most important features of these operations were making the tools of terror accessible to individuals and advertising new freedom to kill. Thousands of placards were placed on billboards and buildings inviting people to avenge their personal wrongs. At meetings organized by the military, high ranking Red Army officers were telling people to "murder and take away the possessions of those who filled their pockets and granaries from your toil and sweat. Where you cannot cope alone the Red Army under the command of our Comrade Stalin will help you." Guns and ammunition were made available to those who wanted to kill against whomever they had a personal grudge—such was the beginning social order under the totalitarian rule.

People were continually encouraged to denounce anybody they wanted to see arrested and destroyed. Once it became generally known that one could turn anybody in, without any questions asked, and without any proof required for a report, criteria by which people found themselves arrested and deported were fluid and many. Even the name of the person denouncing another one didn't have to be disclosed—all the NKVD wanted was the name of the intended victim. Under the totalitarian system, everyone is helpless in ensuring his own personal safety.

And on the other hand, everybody is powerful enough to decide about life or death of almost anyone of his fellow citizens. That is the general idea of social equalization in totalitarianism.

I myself laughed and, at the same time, could not help feeling cold shivers going down my spine when some Russian prisoners, including my friend Alyosha, said that many Russian people keep a bundle of spare clothes at home, in case of arrest, which is called "equalizing" everybody. Social atomization means reducing each individual's loyalty to only the state and not to the family or one's marital partner. This is one of the main characteristics of totalitarianism. It is brought about by this privatization of the system of terror, forcing loyalty to the state by using fear. It does not happen because one party liquidates all other organizations, but comes from the fact that people are afraid of one another. It is in the nature of social relationships, that people can only do evil to others, but they are unable to defend themselves against an attack by another person. At any time, a citizen can use the state against another citizen. Yet there is no way for a citizen to defend himself against an attack from the government (secret police), because the individual is always subservient to the state.

Totalitarianism is realized only when people living and working together no longer see the commonality of their individual interests. Mutual distrust, or even personal hatred for another person, is the surest mainstay of the Soviet power and authority. Thus the essence of totalitarianism, or the source from which the Soviet system derives itself, is the evil and fear that dwells in man. Soviet propaganda for years has been, unintentionally perhaps, complimenting human nature, by repetitively bragging about their efforts to reforge human nature, so that sooner or later they could have a man totally devoted to the Soviet system. A true Soviet man, the *Homo sovieticus* is not the *Homo sapiens*, nor *Homo faber*, but a being estranged from human society. He stands apart from his own society, his neighbor, and, ultimately, himself. It is dangerous for him to develop close personal relationships or speak his true observations and thoughts, because they could turn him in. He has been degraded, debased, and has ended up with a broken-up character, looking around with jaundiced eyes at those around him who have not yet proven themselves disloyal to their own beliefs.

The final result of the Soviet system, applied to nations that were once free, is the world described by George Orwell (Eric Blair) in his books *Animal Farm: A Fairy Story* (1945) and *Nineteen Eighty-four* (1949). The scenarios in these books have not yet come to full fruition. However, if Russian expansionism continues to proceed unchecked, our children may be forced to live in the world of *1984* by the year 2084.

Soviet totalitarianism is a social system begotten by a group of individuals who witnessed a great deal of inhuman brutality done to them or to their loved ones. Their lives' ambition was revenge on a grand scale, which has gotten out of control and spread like wildfire or an incurable cancer. This monstrous Frankenstein of a society can only be returned to its human image, in my humble opinion, if its component members are helped and reinforced in their desire to be free again. They need help from their brothers and sisters who live in societies that are still free. Let the truth be told about the atrocities and barbarism perpetrated upon people behind the Iron Curtain. Let us not believe those grand masters of deceit. Let the history of Russian relationships with other nations be taught at all levels of our educational process.

Let us watch out for the Soviet agents who are anxiously planting the germs of dissent within our society. Such a communicable disease in our neighbor's house should also concern us. Ignorance of the past and how these evils are spread will only do disservice to ourselves and to our future generations. The purpose of this essay is not to forment trouble or cause alarm, but only to raise awareness of methods being used by the Russians to advance their cause. In the U.S., the Nazis have been promoted as the greatest threat to freedom that mankind has ever experienced. Yet few know or really care to acknowledge that Russian expansionism is just as serious a threat, though not as immediate (but longer in span). The real threat is to our freedom as individuals. Individual freedom and the rights of the individual, combined with the Golden Rules ("Do unto others as you would have them do unto you," and "Love thy neighbor as thyself") will eventually bring about peace on our planet. But until it is clearly illustrated in action on both sides, for many, many years, we should not drop our guard against the evil in Russian expansion.

Mr. Gorbachev is perceived by many throughout the world to be a benevolent leader with the well-being of his people and the world foremost in mind. So far, *Glasnost* and *Perestroika* have stimulated much discussion throughout the world. However, "the old guard" is still in power through the local party bosses. *Perestroika* has not made its way down to the people standing in line for food and clothing, nor to the people still suffering and dying in prison camps. Openness and restructuring have not yet resulted in broad social changes. They are still mostly just good ideas that need to be fully translated into actions that benefit the economies of Soviet societies.

It is clear that Mr. Gorbachev's short-term vision for

Russia is to pull it out of its deepest economic woes since the Russian Revolution and to eventually establish it as a major economic power. It is not clear whether his long-term vision is to go with the flow of four-hundred-plus years of expansionism or a grander vision to free the hearts, souls, and minds of the Russian people. His unwillingness to yield on human rights violations is an indication of the former.

CHRONOLOGY OF COMMUNIST (RUSSIAN) IMPERIALISM

The list below includes only the major examples of Russian imperialism until 1984. It is not be claimed that it is complete and all-inclusive. The Russian invasions and conquests have not all been of the military type, therefore, they could not all be identified right away.

The First Five Years

1917—Soviet Communist State created in Russia on November 8, 1917, following the Bolshevik coup d'etat that overthrew the Provisional Government headed by Anatole Kerensky.
1919—Armenia, Azerbaidzhan, Bielarus, Georgia, Kazakhstan, Mongolia, Ukraine, all occupied by Soviet Russia.
1922—Russia renamed the Union of Soviet Socialist Republics in December.

At the Beginning of World War II

1939—Eastern Poland .... Annexed by USSR.
1940—Eastern Romania and northern East Prussia .... Annexed by USSR.
1940—Estonia, Latvia and Lithuania...Annexed by USSR.

World War II and Its Aftermath

1944—Poland, Bulgaria, and Romania colonized by USSR.
1944—Eastern Finland and Tannu-Tuva annexed by USSR.
1944—Hungary .... Colonized by USSR.
1945—Eastern Germany .... Colonized by the USSR.
1945—North Korea .... Puppet state of USSR.
1945—Kurile Islands and Sakhalin Island. Annexed by USSR.
1948—Czechoslovakia .... Colonized by USSR.
1948—East Berlin colonized by East Germany and USSR.
1949—Yugoslavia .... Left Soviet Bloc, still Communist.
1948/49—China .... Client state of USSR.

Decades of the Fifties and Sixties

1950/52— North Korea invaded South Korea. Invasion failed.
1954—North Vietnam ..... Client state of USSR and China.
1956—Hungary Freedom Fighters crushed, recolonized by USSR.
1959—Cuba .... Puppet state of USSR.
1960/62—China .... Left Soviet Bloc; still Communist.
1962—Albania .... Left Soviet Bloc; still Communist.
1968—Czechoslovakia Reformers ousted, recolonized by USSR.

Decades of the Seventies and Eighties

1975/76 — Angola and Mozambique .... Colonized by Cuba and USSR.
1977/78 — Ethiopia .... Colonized by Cuba and USSR.
1977/78 — South Yemen .... Puppet state of USSR.
1978 — Afghanistan .... Colonized by Cuba and USSR.
1979/80 — Nicaragua .... Puppet state of Cuba and USSR.
1979/80 — Afghanistan .... Invaded and colonized by USSR.
1981 — Poland Solidarity Movement crushed. Recolonized by USSR.
1980 — Suriname .... Puppet state of Cuba.
1983 — Grenada ....Liberated.
1989 — Afghanistan USSR retreated, left country in severe disarray, puppet government in control.